Strategies for Literacy Education

Katherine D. Wiesendanger
Alfred University

Merrill
Prentice Hall

Upper Saddle River, New Jersey
Columbus, Ohio

Library of Congress Cataloging-in-Publication Data

Wiesendanger, Katherine.
  Strategies for literacy education / Katherine D. Wiesendanger.
     p. cm.
  Includes index.
  ISBN 0-13-022148-1
  1. Language arts (Elementary) 2. Curriculum planning. 3. Elementary school
teachers—In-service training. I. Title.

LB1576.W4875 2001
372.6—dc21   99-086305

Vice President and Publisher: Jeffery W. Johnston
Editor: Bradley J. Potthoff
Production Editor: Mary M. Irvin
Design Coordinator: Diane C. Lorenzo
Cover Design: Jeff Vanik
Cover Art: SuperStock
Production Manager: Pamela D. Bennett
Editorial Assistant: Jennifer Day
Editorial Production Supervision and Text Design: Amy Gehl, Carlisle Publishers Services
Director of Marketing: Kevin Flanagan
Marketing Manager: Amy June
Marketing Services Manager: Krista Groshong

This book was set in Palatino by Carlisle Publishers Services and was printed and bound by R. R. Donnelley &
Sons Company. The cover was printed by Phoenix Color Corporation.

Merrill
Prentice Hall

10 9 8 7 6 5 4 3 2 1
ISBN: 0-13-022148-1

Preface

PURPOSE OF THIS BOOK

Teachers understand the issues of accountability and want to advance and develop professionally. They have a perpetual need for strategies to assist them in planning curricular objectives, yet great demands on their time make it difficult for them to plan such strategies. Commercially prepared materials may offer excellent suggestions but may not allow teachers to meet the specific demands of the classroom such as dealing with individual differences. Teachers want alternative strategies and ideas to ensure their objectives are met for all students.

This book was written to provide a resource for teachers and to give them a selection of interesting and stimulating strategies that will assist them in developing lessons helpful for students' advancement in reading. These strategies are designed to motivate and encourage reading and should prove useful to both preservice and inservice teachers in improving the teaching-learning process and planning for appropriate instruction. They should help teachers evaluate the literacy needs of students and plan lessons accordingly. By working through the strategies in this book, teachers can help children achieve goals.

The text is not theoretical, nor does it attempt to justify a particular reading theory. The assumption is that one has developed a theoretical framework about literacy before using these strategies. The strategies, however, are based on sound research and were selected because they can be used with any reading program. They are manageable, of high interest, easy to implement, and adaptable.

WHO SHOULD USE THIS BOOK?

Both preservice and inservice teachers will find the strategies in the text useful. The text is ideal to use with classes that contain a practicum component. Student teachers can use the text as a general guide. Preservice teachers can use the strategies to develop lessons and apply them to concepts presented in a theoretical text. If preservice teachers are engaged in tutoring students, they can design lessons for different ability groups or try to incorporate several of the strategies in each of the five major areas of the text.

Inservice teachers can use this book as an alternative to commercialized instruction and workbook pages. The strategies will enable them to incorporate variety into their classrooms and help motivate students by keeping them active and attentive. Teachers can sharpen their expertise in what is effective with different groups of students, as well as design and implement lessons that would best suit the students' needs. Finally, they can use this book to develop both alternative and reinforcement activities for the wide range of students within their classrooms.

CONTENT OF THIS BOOK

The text is divided into five major sections: word identification, meaning vocabulary, comprehension, writing, and study skills.

Word Identification. This section is devoted to providing strategies for those students who need more experience with the printed word because they have an inadequate sight vocabulary, problems with decoding, or problems with structural analysis.

Meaning Vocabulary. This section consists mainly of strategies that allow teachers to develop lessons for students who lack the ability to understand underlying concepts. These strategies help teachers plan lessons in which students interpret concepts necessary for understanding connected text. They incorporate dialogue, explanations, descriptions, and experiences into the lessons.

Comprehension. These strategies enable students who have difficulty constructing messages from the printed text. They have an interactive approach and focus on the process of metacognition, consequently helping students learn how to learn.

Writing. The strategies in this section emphasize the writing process. With these strategies, students can learn from text by integrating reading and writing. Many of the strategies in other sections of the text also could incorporate a writing component. The creation of a separate writing category does not imply that the reading-writing process should not be integrated. Rather, its purpose is to provide teachers with strategies directed toward writing. When selecting strategies, teachers should be mindful of the importance of connecting reading and writing. They also should stress the processes of writing as well as the integration of the curriculum.

Study Skills. These strategies help teachers develop lessons to help students learn more effectively by enabling them to acquire information from the text. They are mainly intended for use with expository text.

The strategies incorporated in each of these categories have been implemented successfully in the classroom. They are designed to help teachers develop lessons by giving them ideas they could use in the classroom. While specific steps are given for each strategy, teachers are encouraged to develop variations for meeting individual needs.

The following information is presented for each strategy:

Desired Outcome explains the purpose or overall goal in using the strategy.

General Overview gives a brief summary of the strategy and often includes such information as under what specific circumstances a teacher might use the strategy to help ensure success.

Steps Used in the Strategy outlines the procedure for using the strategy, using clear instructions on how to use each strategy when designing a lesson. Specific directions are given to enable the teacher to implement the strategy and adapt it to suit the lesson's objectives.

Additional Information includes pertinent knowledge that may be useful when designing a lesson. This section focuses on suggestions for modifying the strategy and alternative suggestions to consider when implementing the strategy.

Charts and diagrams may be included at the end of each chapter as examples of how the strategy might best be implemented. These visuals will enable teachers to conceptualize their final outcome and understand how students can show their interactions with the text.

FINAL CONSIDERATIONS

Reading is a complex process and needs to be developed and taught both holistically and systematically. Teachers should make the act of reading comfortable and nonthreatening for all students in order that they may develop intrinsic motivators and be continually successful.

While the procedures for implementing the strategies are presented step by step as in a typical lesson plan format, the intent is not to oversimplify the teaching of reading by implying that teaching is a prescriptive process. Consequently, teachers are encouraged either to use the strategies in their entirety or to adapt them to meet the needs of the specific situation. As teachers become more familiar with the strategies and more proficient in incorporating them into their curriculum, they are encouraged to combine several strategies in one lesson and adapt them to fit the lesson's objectives, students' needs, and environmental constraints.

Keeping in mind that the most effective lessons often integrate the curriculum, relate it to the realities of students' lives, and incorporate several organizational or grouping patterns, knowledgeable teachers should take the substance of each strategy and adapt, modify, or elaborate it as necessary.

Finally, teachers can use this text as a resource or reference guide for implementing the ideas and strategies with different types of children in various educational contexts. Teachers can use this text to expand and develop their own style and to accommodate the ever-increasing and more complicated needs of their students.

ACKNOWLEDGMENTS

I wish to thank the many teachers and graduate students who were instrumental in the preparation of this manuscript. Hundreds of professionals gave concrete and realistic suggestions about the instructional strategies used in this text. Particular appreciation is due to Lori Cambareri.

Special thanks goes to Mary Evangelista, who did an excellent job in preparing the manuscript for production, and Brad Potthoff, the sponsoring editor, who gave me unique insight from the beginning to the end of the project.

Appreciation is also given to the reviewers of the manuscript who contributed significantly to the finished product: Denise M. Bartelo, Plymouth State College of New Hampshire; Carole L. Bond, University of Memphis; William Oehlkers, Rhode Island College; Lorelie Olson, Seattle Pacific University; Daniel L. Pearce, Texas A & M University–Corpus Christi; David G. Petkosh, Cabrini College; Elaine Roberts, State University of West Georgia; and Gary D. Spray, California State University, Sacramento.

Discover the Companion Website Accompanying This Book

THE PRENTICE HALL COMPANION WEBSITE: A VIRTUAL LEARNING ENVIRONMENT

Technology is a constantly growing and changing aspect of our field that is creating a need for content and resources. To address this emerging need, Prentice Hall has developed an online learning environment for students and professors alike—Companion Websites—to support our textbooks.

In creating a Companion Website, our goal is to build on and enhance what the textbook already offers. For this reason, the content for each user-friendly website is organized by topic and provides the professor and student with a variety of meaningful resources. Common features of a Companion Website include:

FOR THE PROFESSOR

Every Companion Website integrates **Syllabus Manager**™, an online syllabus creation and management utility.

- **Syllabus Manager**™ provides you, the instructor, with an easy, step-by-step process to create and revise syllabi, with direct links into Companion Website and other online content without having to learn HTML.
- Students may log on to your syllabus during any study session. All they need to know is the web address for the Companion Website and the password you've assigned to your syllabus.
- After you have created a syllabus using **Syllabus Manager**™, students may enter the syllabus for their course section from any point in the Companion Website.

- Clicking on a date, the student is shown the list of activities for the assignment. The activities for each assignment are linked directly to actual content, saving time for students.
- Adding assignments consists of clicking on the desired due date, then filling in the details of the assignment—name of the assignment, instructions, and whether or not it is a one-time or repeating assignment.
- In addition, links to other activities can be created easily. If the activity is online, a URL can be entered in the space provided, and it will be linked automatically in the final syllabus.
- Your completed syllabus is hosted on our servers, allowing convenient updates from any computer on the Internet. Changes you make to your syllabus are immediately available to your students at their next log on.

FOR THE STUDENT

- **Topic Overviews**–outline key concepts in topic areas
- **Electronic Blue Book**–send homework or essays directly to your instructor's email with this paperless form
- **Message Board**–serves as a virtual bulletin board to post—or respond to—questions or comments to/from a national audience
- **Chat**–real-time chat with anyone who is using the text anywhere in the country—ideal for discussion and study groups, class projects, etc.
- **Web Destinations**–links to www sites that relate to each topic area
- **Professional Organizations**–links to organizations that relate to topic areas
- **Additional Resources**–access to topic-specific content that enhances material found in the text

To take advantage of these and other resources, please visit the *Strategies for Literacy Education* Companion Website at **www.prenhall.com/wiesendanger**

Contents

Introduction: How to Use This Book   1

Chapter 1   Word Identification Strategies   7

  1.1 The Bag Game   8
  1.2 Basic Function Words   9
  1.3 DSTA (Directed Spelling Thinking Activity)   10
  1.4 Inductive Phonics   13
  1.5 Making Words   15
  1.6 Paired Repeated Reading   17
  1.7 Progressive Cloze   19
  1.8 Sound Isolation Used to Develop Phonemic Awareness   21
  1.9 Sticker Books   23
  1.10 Support-Reading   23
  1.11 Synthetic Phonics   24
  1.12 Talking Books   25
  1.13 Thematic Word Wall   26
  1.14 VLP (Vocabulary, Language, Prediction)   27
  1.15 Vocabulary Self-Collection   29
  1.16 Word Analogies   31

1.17 Word Building   34

1.18 Word Cluster   35

1.19 Word Expansions   39

1.20 Word Sort   39

1.21 Word Storm   40

Chapter 2   Meaning Vocabulary Strategies   43

2.1 Adjective/Verb/Noun Word Maps   44

2.2 Big Books   45

2.3 Capsules   49

2.4 Cloze Instruction   50

2.5 Conceptual Mapping   50

2.6 Contextual Processing   52

2.7 Contextual Redefinition   56

2.8 ELVES (Excite, Listen, Visualize, Extend, and Savor)   57

2.9 GRIP (Generative Reciprocal Instructional Procedure)   58

2.10 Keywords   59

2.11 List-Group-Label (LGL)   60

2.12 Literature Circles   61

2.13 Marginal Glosses   63

2.14 Motor Imaging   64

2.15 Possible Sentences   64

2.16 Predict-O-Gram   65

2.17 Pyramid   66

2.18 Semantic Feature Analysis   68

2.19 TOAST (Test, Organize, Anchor, Say, and Test)   71

2.20 Visual Guessing Game   75

Chapter 3 *Comprehension Strategies*   77

3.1 Anticipation Guide   78

3.2 Captioned Video   79

3.3 Character Analysis   82

3.4 Choral Reading   82

3.5 Creating an Animated Film Story   84

3.6 Discussion Web   85

3.7 DRTA (Directed Reading-Thinking Activity)   86

3.8 Episodic Mapping   88

3.9 Find the Features   91

3.10 Guided Reading Procedure   93

3.11 Guide-O-Rama   94

3.12 Informal Books   96

3.13 InQuest (Investigative Questioning)   97

3.14 Jigsaw Method   98

3.15 KWLA (What I Already *Know*; What I *Want* to Know;
     What I *Learned*; and the *Affect* of the Story)   99

3.16 KWL-Plus   100

3.17 Linguistic Roulette   104

3.18 Playing About a Story   105

3.19 Portfolios   105

3.20 Prediction Book Report   106

3.21 Pyramiding   107

3.22 QAR (Question-Answer Relationship)   108

3.23 Read Aloud   111

3.24 Reading Place   111

3.25 Repeated Reading   112

3.26 ReQuest   113

3.27 RMA (Retrospective Miscue Analysis)   114

3.28 Semantic Mapping   116

3.29 Shared Book Experience   120

3.30 SSR (Sustained Silent Reading)   120

3.31 Story Character Map   121

3.32 Story Impressions   122

3.33 Story Frames   124

3.34 Story Retelling   127

3.35 Story Writing Map   130

3.36 Summarization   131

3.37 TELLS Fact or Fiction   131

3.38 Thematic Experience   132

3.39 Think Alouds   134

3.40 Visual Comprehension   135

3.41 Webbing   136

Chapter 4   *Writing Strategies*   139

4.1 3W2H   140

4.2 Buddy Journals   141

4.3 Curious George   142

4.4 Double-Entry Reading Journals   144

4.5 Elaboration   144

4.6 Graphic Organizer—Venn Diagram   147

4.7 Group Summarizing   149

4.8 Kinderjournals   151

4.9 Middle School Picture Books   153

4.10 Probable Passages   154

4.11 QUIP (Questions Into Paragraphs)   155

4.12 Reviewing a Film   157

4.13 Sentence Collecting   159

4.14 Storyboard Technique   161

4.15 Wordless Picture Books   161

4.16 ZigZag   163

Chapter 5   *Study Skills Strategies*   167

5.1 Five-Day Test Preparation Plan   168

5.2 Basis for Outlining   168

5.3 Circle of Questions   169

5.4 CSM (Cloze Story Mapping)   170

5.5 Collaborative Learning   173

5.6 Cooperative Group Rotation   175

5.7 Directed Inquiry Activity   177

5.8 DRTA+SQ (Directed Reading Thinking Activity and Student Question)   178

5.9 FLIP (Friendliness, Language, Interest, Prior Knowledge)   180

5.10 Information Charts   181

5.11 Intuitive Reading   183

5.12 Jot Charts   183

5.13 OH RATS (Overview, Headings, Read, Answer, Test-Study)   185

5.14 Previewing Books   187

5.15 PSRT (Prepare, Structure, Read, and Think)   188

5.16 Reciprocal Teaching   189

5.17 SCAIT (Select, Complete, Accept, Infer, and Think)   190

5.18 The Scientific Method   191

5.19 Selective Reading Guide-O-Rama   193

5.20 SQ3R (Survey, Question, Read, Recite, and Review)   194

5.21 S2RAT (Select, Review, Return, Assign, and Test)   195
5.22 Text Preview   196
5.23 Text Structure   197
5.24 Underlining   199
5.25 Wagon Wheels   200

References   203

Index   207

Introduction: How to Use this Book

While there are several important variables in determining the students' success, the teacher is one of the most significant. Some teachers are more capable of helping students achieve results in literacy than are others. These successful teachers know that teaching reading is a very complicated process. They have developed an understanding of literacy and a sound theoretical philosophy. The strategies in this book should enable these teachers to apply theory to practical situations and, thus, maintain a classroom environment that fosters learning.

Before selecting an appropriate strategy, teachers need to consider a number of variables. The long- and short-term goals for the group or individual students should be the first consideration in lesson development. Goals of the lesson should be knowledge, skills, or performances the children have not yet attained but are ready to achieve. The curriculum and the students' problems and strengths are factors used to determine these goals. After studying these factors, the teacher should establish the objective(s) of the lesson and confirm the knowledge, understanding, skills, or performances children might attain or develop as a result of the lesson.

After determining the lesson's goals, a second consideration might be how students should be grouped in order to achieve them. The teacher must decide if the lesson elements lend themselves to whole, small, or pupil partner grouping arrangements or if the grouping should include students of similar or different academic abilities. To determine this, the teacher should take into account the grade level, range of abilities, and personalities of the students and should decide the number of grouping patterns appropriate for the lesson. For example, the teacher might interact initially with the entire class as a whole unit, continue in smaller groups or with pupil partners for the second phase of the lesson, and conclude the lesson with yet a third grouping arrangement.

It is imperative that these decisions guide the selection of the strategy, rather than having the strategy become an end in itself or dictate the lesson. Once these decisions are made, it is appropriate to select those strategies that coincide with the lesson's objective, grouping procedures, and classroom environment. Only after the teacher has determined relevant critical information, is she able to select the best strategy for achieving the lesson's desired outcome. Keeping the objective(s) in mind, the next step in the process is to develop several related activities that would enable the students to achieve them.

In order to correlate the strategies with the specific text or information that is to be taught, it is helpful to refer to both the book's table of contents and the grid. Basically, the teacher must select a specific category and examine those strategies placed within it.

In the table of contents, the strategies are divided into five broad areas, which include word identification, meaning vocabulary, comprehension, writing, and study skills strategies. In order for the teacher to choose the area that best coincides with the strategy type needed, he might ask questions similar to the following. Would students benefit from a visual representation of ideas? Will children have to compare/contrast different characters from the text? Must children learn to identify a number of words before they are able to read the selection? Is it appropriate to develop vocabulary concepts to which children must relate in order to understand the author's underlying message? Is it appropriate to integrate a writing strategy into the literacy lesson? Do study skills need to be improved?

PURPOSE AND PROCEDURE FOR USING THE GRID

While each strategy has been designated under one of the preceding categories, it is difficult sometimes to obtain a precise indication of the chapter's contents from the title alone. To compensate for this, a grid has been included which gives specific information about each strategy. This additional information should prove useful when selecting a strategy. The grid is organized as an overview. In the first column, one can determine whether the strategy is best used with groups of students, pupil partners, or individual students. The second column indicates whether the strategy is most appropriate for prereading, during reading, or postreading. A final column indicates the grade level for which the activity would be most appropriate.

It is important to note that the purpose of these columns is only to offer suggestions. Classrooms and the individual students that comprise those classrooms all have unique characteristics and can differ dramatically in an array of variables. Therefore, teachers should determine which strategies would be most appropriate for the children in their classroom.

After selecting a category, the teacher might refer to the grid for guidelines as to the appropriateness of using each strategy. The strategies are arranged here as in the table of contents. Their names and page numbers are listed in the first two columns. In the third, teachers receive information on when in the lesson to implement the strategy. If the strategy is to be used before children read the material, it is coded with a *B*. If it is more appropriate to use during the process of reading, it is coded with a *D*; if it should be used after reading, it is coded with an *A*.

The fourth column focuses on whether the strategy should be used with expository or narrative text. Expository text is generally referred to as content area material, and the relevant strategies are coded *E.* In contrast, narrative text usually contains story elements, and those appropriate strategies are coded *N.*

The grid's next column includes the concept of grouping. An *I* implies that the strategy might be used when tutoring individuals, while strategies coded with a *P* are appropriate to use with lessons when the teacher wants children to work together with partners. When selecting a strategy for use with a whole group, the teacher should choose one that is coded with a *G.*

The final column indicates the appropriateness of the strategy in relation to grade level. Strategies coded with a *P* are more appropriate for use with primary students, while those coded with an *M* are effective with children in the middle grades; *J* and *H* are designations for junior and senior high, respectively.

	Page Number	B = Before Reading D = During Reading A = After Reading	E = Expository N = Narrative	I = Individual P = Partners G = Group	Grade Level E = Early Elementary M = Middle Elementary U = Upper Elementary H = High School A = All
1.1 The Bag Game	8	B		P	E
1.2 Basic Function Words	9	B		I, P, G	E, M
1.3 DSTA	10	A	E	I, G	E
1.4 Inductive Phonics	13	B, A		I	E
1.5 Making Words	15	B		I, P, G	E, M
1.6 Paired Repeated Reading	17	D	E, N	P	E, M, U
1.7 Progressive Cloze	19	D	N	I, P, G	A
1.8 Sound Isolation	21	B, A	E, N	P, G	E, M
1.9 Sticker Books	23	D	N	I, P, G	E, M
1.10 Support-Reading	23	B, D, A	N	P, G	E, M
1.11 Synthetic Phonics	24	B		I, G	E, M
1.12 Talking Books	25	D	N	I, P, G	
1.13 Thematic Word Wall	26	B	E, N	G	A
1.14 VLP	27	B	E, N	I, G	M, U, H
1.15 Vocabulary Self-Collection	29	B	E, N	G	A
1.16 Word Analogies	31	B, A			
1.17 Word Building	34	B, A		I, P	E, M
1.18 Word Cluster	35	B, A	E, N	I, P, G	
1.19 Word Expansions	39	B, A		I, P, G	E, M
1.20 Word Sort	39	B		I, P, G	E, M
1.21 Word Storm	40	B		P, G	E, M, U
2.1 Adjective/Verb/Noun Maps	44	B	E, N	I, P, G	E, M, U
2.2 Big Books	45	B, D, A	N	G	E
2.3 Capsules	49	B	E, N	P, G	M, U, H

	Page Number	B = Before Reading D = During Reading A = After Reading	E = Expository N = Narrative	I = Individual P = Partners G = Group	Grade Level E = Early Elementary M = Middle Elementary U = Upper Elementary H = High School A = All
2.4 Cloze Instruction	50	D	E, N	I, P, G	A
2.5 Conceptual Mapping	50	B, A	E, N	P, G	A
2.6 Contextual Processing	52	D	E, N	P, G	M, U, H
2.7 Contextual Redefinition	56	B		I, P, G	A
2.8 ELVES	57	D	N	I, G	E
2.9 GRIP	58	B	N	I, G	A
2.10 Keywords	59	B	N	I, G	M, U, H
2.11 List-Group-Label	60	B, A	E	I, P	A
2.12 Literature Circles	61	A	N	G	A
2.13 Marginal Glosses	63	D	E	I	M, U, H
2.14 Motor Imaging	64	B	E, N	G	E, M
2.15 Possible Sentences	64	B	E	G	
2.16 Predict-O-Gram	65	B	N	I, P, G	A
2.17 Pyramid	66	A	N	I, P, G	U, H
2.18 Semantic Feature Analysis	68	B, A	E	P, G	A
2.19 TOAST	71	B, A	E, N	I, P, G	A
2.20 Visual Guessing Game	75	B	E, N	G	E
3.1 Anticipation Guide	78	B, A	E, N	I, P, G	M, U, H
3.2 Captioned Video	79	B, A	N	G	E, M
3.3 Character Analysis	82	A	N	G	A
3.4 Choral Reading	82	D	E, N	G	E, M
3.5 Creating an Animated Film	84	B, A	E, N	G	U, H
3.6 Discussion Web	85	A	E, N	G	A
3.7 DRTA	86	B, D, A	E, N	I, P, G	E, M, U
3.8 Episodic Mapping	88	B, A	E, N	I, P, G	A
3.9 Find the Features	91	B, A	N	I, P, G	M, U, H
3.10 Guided Reading Procedure	93	D	E	I	A
3.11 Guide-O-Rama	94	D	E	I	M, U, S
3.12 Informal Books	96	D	N	I, G	E
3.13 InQuest	97	D	N	I, G	M, U, H
3.14 Jigsaw Method	98	D	E	G	M, U, H
3.15 KWLA	99	B, D, A	E	I, P, G	A
3.16 KWL-Plus	100	B, D, A	E	I, P, G	M, U, H
3.17 Linguistic Roulette	104	A	N	G	U, H
3.18 Playing About a Story	105	A	N	G	E
3.19 Portfolios	105	A			A
3.20 Prediction Book Report	106	D	E	I	M, U, H
3.21 Pyramiding	107	A	N	I, P, G	A

	Page Number	B = Before Reading D = During Reading A = After Reading	E = Expository N = Narrative	I = Individual P = Partners G = Group	Grade Level E = Early Elementary M = Middle Elementary U = Upper Elementary H = High School A = All
3.22 QAR	108	B, A	E, N	I	M, U, H
3.23 Read Aloud	111	D	E, N	P	A
3.24 Reading Place	111	D	E	I, G	E, M
3.25 Repeated Reading	112	D	E, N	G	E, M
3.26 ReQuest	113	B, D, A	E, N	I, G	M, U, H
3.27 RMA	114	D, A	N	I	A
3.28 Semantic Mapping	116	B, A	E, N	I, G	A
3.29 Shared Book Experience	120	B, D, A	N	G	E, M
3.30 SSR: Sustained Silent Reading	120	D	N	I	A
3.31 Story Character Map	121	D, A	N	I	M, U, H
3.32 Story Impressions	122	B, A	N	G	A
3.33 Story Frames	124	A	N	I, P, G	A
3.34 Story Retelling	127	A	N	I, P, G	M, U, H
3.35 Story Writing Map	130	B	N	I	M, U, H
3.36 Summarization	131	A	N	I, P	A
3.37 TELLS Fact or Fiction	131	B, A	N	I, P, G	A
3.38 Thematic Experience	132	B, D, A	E, N	I, P, G	A
3.39 Think Alouds	134	D	E, N	I	M, U, H
3.40 Visual Comprehension	135	D	N	I	E, M
3.41 Webbing	136	B	N	I, G	M, U, H
4.1 3W2H	140	B	E	I, P, G	M, U, H
4.2 Buddy Journals	141	B, A		P	A
4.3 Curious George	142	B, D, A	N	I, G	E
4.4 Double-Entry Reading Journals	144	A	E	I	M, U, H
4.5 Elaboration	144			I	M, U, H
4.6 Graphic Organizer	147	B, A	E, N	I, P, G	A
4.7 Group Summarizing	149	B, A	E, N	G	M, U, H
4.8 Kinderjournals	151	B, A	E, N	G	E
4.9 Middle School Picture Books	153	A	E	I, P	U, H
4.10 Probable Passages	154	B, A	N	I	M, U, H
4.11 QUIP	155	B, A	E	I, G	M, U, H
4.12 Reviewing a Film	157	B	N	G	M, U, H
4.13 Sentence Collecting	159	A	N	I, P, G	E, M
4.14 Storyboard Technique	161	B		I, G	E
4.15 Wordless Picture Books	161	D	N	G	E
4.16 ZigZag	163	A	E	I, P, G	M, U, H
5.1 Five-Day Test Preparation Plan	168	A	E	I	M, U, H
5.2 Basis for Outlining	168	A	E	I	M, U, H

	Page Number	B = Before Reading D = During Reading A = After Reading	E = Expository N = Narrative	I = Individual P = Partners G = Group	Grade Level E = Early Elementary M = Middle Elementary U = Upper Elementary H = High School A = All
5.3 Circle of Questions	169	A	E, N	I, G	A
5.4 CSM Cloze Story Map	170	A	E	I, P, G	M, U
5.5 Collaborative Learning	173	B, D, A	E, N	P, G	U, H
5.6 Cooperative Group Rotation	175	B, A	E	G	M, U, H
5.7 Directed Inquiry Activity	177	B	E	I, G	M, U, H
5.8 DRTA + SQ	178	B, D, A	E, N	I, P, G	M, U, H
5.9 FLIP	180	B	E	I	M, U, H
5.10 Information Charts	181	B, D, A	E	I	M, U, H
5.11 Intuitive Reading	183	B	N	I, P	E
5.12 Jot Charts	183	D, A	E	I	M, U, H
5.13 OH RATS	185	B, D, A	E	I, P	M, U, H
5.14 Previewing Books	187	B	E	I, G	A
5.15 PSRT	188	B, D, A	E	I, G	U, H
5.16 Reciprocal Teaching	189	B, A	E	P	M, U, H
5.17 SCAIT	190	D, A	E	I, P, G	U, H
5.18 The Scientific Method	191	B, D, A	E	I	U, H
5.19 Selective Reading	193	D, A	E	I, P, G	M, U, H
5.20 SQ3R	194	B, D, A	E	I, P	M, U, H
5.21 S2RAT	195	B	E	I	M, U, H
5.22 Text Preview	196	P	E, N	I, G	M, U, H
5.23 Text Structure	197	D	E, N	G	M, U, H
5.24 Underlining	199	D, A	E, N	I, G	M, U, H
5.25 Wagon Wheels	200	B, D, A	E, N	I, P, G	A

Chapter

1

Word Identification Strategies

1.1   THE BAG GAME

Desired Outcome

This game (Lewkowicz, 1994) is used with student partners to help young readers develop phonemic awareness and recognize initial sounds within words. It also helps children expand their meaning vocabulary by relating spoken words to actual objects.

General Overview

The Bag Game requires enough bags large enough for four objects for each child. The object's name should contain the initial consonant sound the children studied previously. This activity is used as a reinforcement. It is particularly motivating for at-risk and beginning students.

Steps Used in the Strategy

1. Select objects whose names start with initial consonants the students have learned.
2. Have the students name the four kinds of objects as you place them into each bag. Each child in a pair has the same objects in her bag. Pair the students and decide on one to be the matcher and one to be the sounder.
3. Instruct the sounder to look into his bag, reach in, select one of the objects, and hide it. Next have him say just the initial consonant sound of the object to the matcher.
4. Next, have the matcher look in her own bag, find the matching object, grasp it, and lift it into full view.
5. Finally, have the sounder raise his object into view to find if they match. If not, clarify the misunderstanding and have them try again.
6. Select another pair of students and repeat the steps. Make sure to keep switching the objects every few rounds to keep attention level high.

Additional Information

Should the sounder or matcher not correctly associate the object and initial sound, the teacher should "stretch" the sound to help: fffffffeather and tttttop. Then the students practice the sound to familiarize themselves with it. The Bag Game can also be played in groups of two for the whole class. It is helpful to switch the bags with other groups to get everyone involved at once.

1.2 BASIC FUNCTION WORDS

Desired Outcome

This strategy (Carbo, 1978; Cunningham, 1979; Jolly, 1981) can be used to help slower readers decipher difficult function words that are similar in appearance to other function words.

General Overview

Function words, otherwise known as service or connecting words (i.e., *when, if, the, where, but*), have little meaning in themselves. When the reader is unable to associate meaning with a word, it is more difficult to learn. By their very nature, function words can be confusing. This strategy enables the reader to bring meaning to function words. It is a seven-step process used with small groups of about six children. Function words should first be presented to the students in isolation, then in context, and finally in isolation again. A maximum of four function words should be taught during one session.

Steps Used in the Strategy

1. Select up to four function words and write each one on individual cards. On the opposite side of the card, write a phrase that includes the word. Give a set of cards to all students and have them place the cards before them.
2. Next, hold up one card and have the students first look at the word, then match their card that has the same word. Say the word aloud several times while the children read it on their card. Introduce each word in a similar fashion.
3. In this step, say each word and have the children hold up the corresponding card. Repeat the words until each child in the group is able to hold up the correct card for each word.
4. Then, have the children spell the words. Select a word and have the children scrutinize the corresponding word card. Next, have them shut their eyes and try to visualize the word as you say it. Then set the cards aside. Dictate the words and circulate among the group to check for correctness. Have the children use the original cards as a reference and correct any errors.
5. At this stage, have students flip their cards, so that the phrases containing the words are in view. Dictate the phrase twice; each time have the students run their fingers under the words. Finally, select students to read the phrases aloud.

6. Include this step if students need reinforcement. Distribute a sheet of simple maze sentences containing the function words and have the students underline the correct word.
7. Finally, flash the cards randomly several times as the students say the words quickly. Partner students to flash the words to each other if additional practice is needed.

Additional Information

Each child can add the new cards learned to a ring and take it home so the parents can practice the words with their child. Students can look through text, such as a newspaper, and circle as many of the words as possible. They should have a card available as a reference if needed. Also, children should read material on their independent reading level in order to reinforce the words.

1.3   DSTA (DIRECTED SPELLING THINKING ACTIVITY)

Desired Outcome

In this strategy (Zutell, 1996), the students hone their word identification and word analysis skills, as well as receive practice with predicting spelling words, and phonemic awareness.

General Overview

DSTA (Directed Spelling Thinking Activity) is a spelling strategy where students make predictions on patterned spelling words, which are words that contain an identical letter pattern. Students discuss their reasoning and revise their predictions of upcoming words on the pretest. They then practice these words through a series of activities. The focus of DSTA is on active, thoughtful problem solving to help students retain and reinforce spelling patterns.

Steps Used in the Strategy

1. *Prediction and discussion.* Begin with a brief spelling test on the list words in patterns. Then, initiate discussion by asking students how they spelled the specific words, what they were thinking about as they generated those spellings, and why they thought the words would be spelled in that way. Have students listen to each other's explanations and decide which spelling is likely to be correct. Next, present the correct spelling of the word. After several words are discussed in this manner, have the students begin to make the connections to the patterns and revise or confirm their guesses about other words.

FIGURE 1 in Strategy 1.2

Basic Function: Cards and Maze Sentences for *When, How,* and *Then*

Front of Card	Reverse
WHEN	When the bell rings, it will be time for lunch.
HOW	How many eggs are left in the carton?
THEN	If you are good while Mom shops, then she will buy you a toy.

FIGURE 2 in Strategy 1.2
Function Words in Context

Name: _____

> **Instructions:** Read the following sentences. Notice that, for some
> words, there are three available choices. Choose which word makes
> the most sense in each sentence. Circle the correct word.

1. I get to go out and play   when / how / then   my room is clean.

2. In math class, I learned   when / how / then   to do long division.

3. I just don't know   when / how / then   my mother always knows what I am up to.

4. If I always take vitamins,   when / how / then   I probably won't get sick.

5. I am going to get my driver's license   when / how / then   I am sixteen.

2. *Assisted word sorting.* Provide further clarification on the patterns through the use of a word-sorting activity. Choose one word from each category to serve as a key for each column. Mix the remaining word cards together. Begin by selecting a card from the deck, pronouncing the word, and showing it to the group. Have students tell under which column the word should go and their reasoning for that placement. For example, if students have studied the "oke" and "ore" letter patterns, words in the deck may include *token, adore, yoke, wore, broken, galore.* The key words could be *snore* and *woke.* As students select words from the deck, they place them in the appropriate column.

snore	**woke**
adore	token
wore	yoke
galore	broken

3. *Word hunting.* Have the students scan through books, class lists, magazines, newspapers, and so on to build their word banks.
4. *Cooperative and individual word sorting.* Allow students to work in pairs; then individually, sorting first combinations of teacher-supplied words; then on their own. See Step 2.
5. *Practice activities.* Have students choose from a variety of activities to practice the words. Include Have-a-Go sheets, Look-Say-Cover, See-Write-Check, and so on.
6. *Measure and record student success.* Do individualized spelling review at the end of the lesson cycle in a peer-checking format.

Additional Information

This strategy works for all students, especially ones who need a structured view of spelling words that have patterns. It is also helpful for learning-disabled students. DSTA is an effective way to analyze words and their various components.

1.4 INDUCTIVE PHONICS

Desired Outcome

The purpose of this strategy (Durkin, 1993) is for students to increase phonemic awareness. Inductive phonics enables readers to learn specific phonemic elements or grapheme-phoneme relationships in order that they may transfer the sound of the element to an unknown word.

General Overview

In order to decipher words not encountered previously, students must be aware of the phonemic elements and associate the letters to the corresponding sound combinations. Before teaching phonics inductively, be certain students have developed a base of words they know by sight. They then use these base words for learning phonics.

Steps Used in the Strategy

1. Select the phonemic element you want to teach (consonant *b*). Students may learn phonemic elements in different sequences. It may be useful to test children to determine unknown grapheme-phoneme elements when working in remedial situations.

   The objective of this lesson would be to learn the grapheme-phoneme correspondence of the consonant *b*.

2. Select words students know by sight that contain the phonemic element (*b*). Present words so that like elements line up one under the other. This helps students visualize the element.

   ball
   bag
   bat
   banana

3. Have children pronounce words. These words have been introduced in previous lessons, and the children should know them by sight.
4. Ask students to note the similarities in each of the words. Students should specify that all words have both identical letter and sound patterns.

   All words start with the letter *b*.
   All words start with the same sound.

5. With the students, develop the rule. The rule should include the letters and their corresponding sound.

   b = b sound as heard in ball

6. Present the child with unknown words containing the phonemic element that is in the objective in order that they may transfer the grapheme-phoneme relationship to all words containing the sound.

   bingo
   bus

   The objective is to make certain the child can transfer the phonic element to pronounce a word not yet encountered. If the child needs help with the part of the word containing the element not yet studied, it is acceptable for you to pronounce that part and then have the child blend the word together.

   b ing o
   bingo

Additional Information

Common phonemic elements to be taught include the following:

consonant sounds:	b c d f g h j k l m n p q r s t v w x y z
long vowel sounds:	a e i o u as in *a*ge, *e*at, *i*ce, *o*de, *u*se
short vowel sounds:	a e i o u as in *a*t, *e*nd, *i*f, *o*dd, *u*s

consonant blends:

bl (blow)	fl (fly)	sc (score)	st (storm)
br (brag)	fr (free)	sk (sky)	sw (swing)
cl (clean)	gl (globe)	sl (sled)	tr (trace)
cr (crop)	gr (grass)	sm (smell)	tw (twist)
dr (drum)	pl (plum)	sn (snip)	scr (script)
dw (dwell)	pr (pray)	sp (space)	str (straw)

consonant digraphs:

sh (she)	ph (phone)
ch (chill, chef)	ng (sing)
th (the, thin)	gh (rough)

vowel digraphs:

oo (cool, cook)

ew (ew)

aw, au (auto, awl)

ou, ow (out, owl)

oi, oy (oil, oyster)

consonant clusters:

ab, ack, ad, ag, am, an, and, ap, ash, at, ay, et, im, in, ing, ish, it, old, op, ot, um, un

ace, ade, ake, ame, ang, ank, ape, ar, ate, ed, em, en, ent, est, id, ido, ig, ip, ock, ong, uck, ud, ug, up, ut

able, ac, aff, all, aw, ec, eck, el(l), ice, ick, if(f), ight, ink, is(s), ob, od, og, on, ook, or, ub, uf(f), ul(l)

age, ale, alk, ane, as(s), ast, ave, eam, eat, es(s), ev, ic, il(l), ind, ite, oke, ol(l), om, one, ore, oss, ost, ove

ait, air, al, are, au, ea, eaf, eal, ear, eas, ee, er, ew, ied, ir, ire, oa, oi, oo, ou, ound, ought, ue, ur, ure, ture

1.5   MAKING WORDS

Desired Outcome

The Making Words strategy (Cunningham & Cunningham, 1992; Cunningham, Hall, & Defee, 1991) promotes phonemic awareness, or children's ability to associate letter-sound relationships in words, thus increasing knowledge of word patterns and helping them to decode.

General Overview

Students using this strategy learn that changing one letter or the sequence of letters in a word can create an entirely different word. They actively participate by using word cards. This strategy should be used for children who would benefit from improved decoding skills. Each child is given some letters that they use to make words. They make 12–15 words, beginning with two-letter words, then three-letter words, and so on, until the final word is made. The final word always includes all the letters students are given.

Steps Used in the Strategy

Teacher Preparation

1. Choose an ending word (this word should be from a unit or from information that the students are familiar with, such as *battery* if you just finished a unit on electricity). Consider the possible tie-ins to the word, such as its endings, vowels, and letter patterns.
2. Make a list of words that can be made from the letters of the final word.
3. Select 12–15 words of varying length that contain the phonic pattern that you intended to emphasize. A phonic pattern consists of two or more letters (at, op, od, em) that are commonly grouped together.
4. Write all the words on index cards and place them in order from shortest to longest. You will need large and small index cards to make the words. Also, ensure that they are placed in an order that emphasizes letter patterns.
5. Put the cards in an envelope. Write on the envelope the words in the order that you will present them, as well as the phonic patterns you will discuss at the end of the lesson.

Teaching Steps

1. Show children the large letter cards by placing them in a highly visible area, such as the chalkboard ledge, and give each child a matching small letter card.
2. Review the names of the letters on the large letter cards, and have the children repeat the name of the corresponding small letter.
3. Write the number of the letters in the shortest word on the board. Example: write "2" if the word has only two letters. If the ending word is *battery*, and a "2" is written on the board, the students would come up with two-letter words such as *at*. Use the word in a sentence.
4. After a child makes the word correctly, using the individual smaller letter cards, make the same word with the large letter cards, so the children can check their work.
5. Continue having them make words. Always increase the number of letters and indicate that number on the board. Use the words in simple sentences. Give them clues as to what words they will try to make.

6. Ask if anyone can figure out what our "last word" is. Have them make it out of the big letters on the board. Have students use all their letters and make the final word.
7. After making all the words, place the cards (from the shortest to the longest word) along the chalk ledge. While children say and spell the words, have children notice specific phonic patterns.
8. Have children use the phonic patterns and make a few new words. Also have them find words with the same phonic patterns in texts and so on throughout the day.

Additional Information

This strategy is a quick, every-pupil response, manipulative lesson in which children stay actively involved. They must listen intently for sounds and select letters that represent those sounds in order to make words.

Writing instruction may be correlated with phonic instruction by using words with the same phonic patterns emphasized in the word identification strategy. Both small and large words that contain the same phonic element should be used when working with students of multi-ability levels.

1.6   PAIRED REPEATED READING

Desired Outcome

The desired outcomes of this strategy (Fitzpatrick, 1994; Juel, 1991; Koskinen & Blum, 1986; Vacca & Padak, 1990) are to improve oral reading, grammar, listening skills, reading fluency, and word identification, while giving students the opportunity to read material in context.

General Overview

Paired Repeated Reading is implemented by pairing two students with different reading abilities. For example, it is effective to pair a sixth grader (who is having difficulty with her oral reading) with a kindergartner. This is an effective strategy to improve self-esteem while reading aloud. It is thought that the child experiencing difficulty with her reading will receive the practice necessary to improve oral reading skills while reading to a younger student. Both students form a bond and have fun while reading.

Steps Used in the Strategy

1. Have each student select a passage for reading (approximately 50 words).
2. Next, allow students to read their passages silently and decide who will be the first reader.

FIGURE 1 in Strategy 1.5
Making Words

Directions: In the following sentences, one or more letters are missing from the final word. From the word list, select the "at derivative" that would complete the sentence correctly.

Word List:

attic	pat	flat	match
rat	mat	batting	scratch
batter	scat	matter	
patting	cats	pats	
battery	chat	bat	

Example: This is like a big mouse.   _ <u>a</u> <u>t</u>.

1. Wrestlers practice on a   _ <u>a</u> <u>t</u>.
2. You hit a baseball with a   _ a <u>t</u>.
3. The top of a table is   _ _ <u>a</u> <u>t</u>.
4. Mice are afraid of   _ <u>a</u> <u>t</u> <u>s</u>.
5. At restaurants, butter comes in   _ <u>a</u> t <u>s</u>.
6. When you stroke a dog, you're   _ _ <u>t</u> <u>t</u> <u>i</u> <u>n</u> <u>g</u> it.
7. The next person in the dugout will be   _ _ <u>t</u> <u>t</u> <u>i</u> <u>n</u> g.
8. When Mom makes a cake, I help stir the   _ <u>a</u> <u>t</u> <u>t</u> <u>e</u> <u>r</u>.
9. "Why are you crying? What's the   _ <u>a</u> <u>t</u> <u>t</u> <u>e</u> <u>r</u>?"
10. "Get away from there, dog! Go on—   _ <u>c</u> <u>a</u> <u>t</u>."
11. My friends and I like to hang out and   _ <u>h</u> <u>a</u> <u>t</u>.
12. One way you can light a fire is to use a   _ _ <u>t</u> <u>c</u> <u>h</u>.
13. If you have an itch, you often   _ _ <u>r</u> <u>a</u> <u>t</u> <u>c</u> <u>h</u>.
14. Most of our old stuff is up in the   _ <u>t</u> <u>t</u> <u>i</u> <u>c</u>.
15. For my remote control car, I need a new   _ _ <u>t</u> <u>t</u> <u>e</u> <u>r</u> <u>y</u>.

3. *Reader:* Have this student read the passage aloud to his partner three times. Encourage readers to ask their partners for help with difficult words. After each reading, instruct them to answer the question, How well did I read? on a self-evaluation sheet.

Listener: Have this student listen to her partner read. After the second and third readings, tell her partner how her reading improved and note this improvement on a listening sheet.

4. After the third reading, instruct students to switch roles and again follow Step 3.

Additional Information

As a modification of this strategy, the students may select different reading passages from their partners. This makes listening to the partner read more interesting and discourages direct comparison of reading proficiencies. This strategy may help students become fluent readers. It's also effective for developing peer relations by using partner grouping.

1.7   PROGRESSIVE CLOZE

Desired Outcome

The Progressive Cloze (Riley, 1986) is a strategy to use when remediating comprehension problems. Students must construct a meaningful passage using the initial sentence as well as the cloze format as a stimulus.

General Overview

Progressive Cloze monitors comprehension and focuses on the relationship of text elements. Children respond by reading, listening, writing, and speaking. Direct instruction helps clarify the appropriateness of word selection.

Steps Used in the Strategy

1. Present a stimulus sentence and delete a section of the word that needs remediation.
2. In this example, the student had difficulty with the "ump" phonogram. Elicit possible responses from students, which should include several alternatives. Write as shown:

The little boy j____.   jump
                          joke

Then insert an additional clue, _ed.

The little boy j___ed.   jump
                              joke

3. Insert the response that fits best.

The little boy *jumped.*

4. Read the entire sentence aloud with the students.
5. Ask, "What might have happened before the little boy jumped?" Student responses vary; write them as shown:

The little boy jumped.
The dog barked.
The door slammed.
Sam's mom caught him sneaking a cookie.

6. Read the responses with the students.
7. Ask the students to choose, or choose for them, a meaningful alternative and write it above (before) the cloze sentence.

The door slammed.
The little boy jumped.

8. Read both sentences with the students to reestablish the context. Then ask, "What might have happened after the boy jumped?" Write responses as shown:

The door slammed.
The little boy jumped.
The little boy's brother ran into the room.
The dog ran outside.

9. Read the responses aloud with the students.
10. Ask the students to choose, or choose for them, one of the alternatives and write it after the cloze sentence:

The door slammed.
The little boy jumped.
The little boy's brother ran into the room.

11. Read the entire passage once again to reestablish the context.
12. Continue the process by supplying additional sentences with carefully chosen deletions.

Additional Information

Progressive Cloze can be used in elementary through high school. This strategy works for any students but works especially well with students who have difficulty with reading comprehension. Progressive Cloze is appropriate for a small group or an individual.

1.8   SOUND ISOLATION USED TO DEVELOP PHONEMIC AWARENESS

Desired Outcome

This strategy (Yopp, 1992) is based on an understanding that speech is composed of a series of individual sounds. Phonemic awareness is both a prerequisite for and a consequence of learning to read.

General Overview

This strategy can be used at any time. It should not be used as a drill or memorization. There should be a sense of playfulness and fun, so that the children engage in phonemic awareness activities. Students can sit in a group to encourage interaction among children.

Steps Used in the Strategy

1. Develop an activity to identify the task being taught—e.g., blending sounds.
2. Consider a developmental way to engage the students in the task—e.g., games, riddles, guessing games, and familiar songs.

For Word Identification Strategy:

1. Decide on a series of words that can be identified through context clues.
2. Write a sentence for each word, leaving the word out of the sentence and replacing it with a blank.
3. Working with the class or with small groups, ask what word might fill the blank. Have students brainstorm possibilities. Discuss how the word could be predicted from context.
4. When students cannot guess, begin giving them pieces of the word—letters that will form individual consonant or vowel sounds. Another way to use this strategy is to give the letter clues in blends that are being focused on in class, incorporating the unit of study into this exercise.

Additional Information

This activity will work well for preschoolers and kindergartners who have not yet been exposed to the alphabet.

Example 1

The girl went into the garden and picked a green _____ .

Brainstorming possibilities:

flower
weed
vine
stalk of grass
plant

Teacher provides letters:

The girl went into the garden and picked a green pl_____ .

Students guess plant.

Example 2

While I was walking down the street, a _____ drove past and splashed mud on me.

Brainstorming possibilities:

car   motorcycle
truck   bike
van   station wagon
minivan   bike
caravan   roller blader

Teacher provides letters:

While I was walking down the street, a tr_____ drove past and splashed mud on me.

1.9   STICKER BOOKS

Desired Outcomes

In this strategy (Higdon, 1987), children gain an understanding of how to use context clues in deciphering new vocabulary words. They also add new words to their sight vocabularies and improve in independent reading.

General Overview

Sticker books use a predictable language pattern, along with picture clues, to help improve the students' sight word vocabularies. They are primarily used with beginning readers who need a lot of sight word practice and extra motivation. These books can help teach many other concepts as well as sight words, including shapes, money, numbers, dinosaurs, and flowers.

Steps Used in the Strategy

1. Select a topic to use as a focus.
2. Collect as many stickers as possible pertaining to that topic.
3. Create a book consisting of about eight pages.
4. Select a predictable sentence which includes the sight word you are attempting to teach and write it on each page.
5. Place the stickers on the table in front of the student.
6. Use the picture clues from the stickers along with students knowledge of letter sounds and the theme of the book, and have the students figure out the word and which sticker belongs with the word.
7. Keep the sticker books handy for students to read and practice with.

Additional Information

These books are excellent for individual tutoring with students who are having trouble understanding how to use context clues. They also require a minimum amount of instruction, allowing the teacher to monitor students individually while giving them a feeling of independence.

1.10   SUPPORT-READING

Desired Outcome

This is a repeated reading strategy (Morris & Nelson, 1992) arranged in a cooperative group fashion, which promotes reading fluency.

General Overview

The Support-Reading strategy contains several fluency instruction elements and is meant to be integrated into traditional classes using basal materials. It follows a three-day instructional cycle that lasts 20–25 minutes at a time. Through the use of echo-reading and repeated partner reading, fluency improves.

Steps Used in the Strategy

1. *Day one.* Read a story to a small group of students in a fluent, expressive voice. Throughout the reading, ask students to clarify text information and predict upcoming events. Then echo-read the story, with the students reading from their own books. Monitor individuals' reading and provide assistance, support, and encouragement as necessary.
2. *Day two.* Divide students into pairs that include a good reader and a less proficient one. The pairs reread the story, alternating pages as they go. Then, assign children a short segment (100 words) from the story. In pairs, have the students read to their partners, who provide help as needed. Finally, if there is enough time remaining, have the pairs reread the entire story, alternating pages so that each child reads the text that was read by her partner in the initial partner reading.
3. *Day three.* During a seat-work period, allow individual children to read their assigned parts to you while you monitor the reading for word recognition accuracy.

Additional Information

The Support-Reading strategy was developed in response to the needs of a group of low-reading second-grade students, but this strategy may be useful for other readers of different ages.

1.11   SYNTHETIC PHONICS

Desired Outcomes

In the Synthetic Phonics strategy (McCutchen, Bell, France, & Perfetti, 1991), students learn to use phonic skills to decode unfamiliar words, thus increasing their word analysis skills.

General Overview

Synthetic phonics is an approach to teaching decoding that proceeds from small parts to entire words. It teaches a number of separate grapheme-phoneme relationships and then teaches children how to combine, or blend, individual sounds in order to recognize a word.

Steps Used in the Strategy

1. Model the blending procedure. Point to each letter separately, indicating the equivalent phoneme for each (c = /k/, u = /u/, t=/t/). Then slide your finger under the first portion of the words (cu) and say this blended sound (/ku/). Slide your finger under the final portion of the word (t) and say this sound (/t/). Slide your finger under the entire word and say the blended sound (/Kut/). Circle the word with your finger and say, "This is the word *cut.*"
2. Have children imitate the model with you. Maintain your use of verbal cues and finger cues to assist them.
3. Repeat Step 2, but do not say either the sounds or the blends. Have students repeat these as you continue the verbal cues and finger cues.
4. Repeat Step 3. This time, also remove the verbal cues, giving only finger cues.
5. Incorporate independent blending practice by having children independently perform the pointing, sounding, and blending steps.

Additional Information

There are three variations of sound blending that can be incorporated with the synthetic phonics approach:

1. The word is sounded letter-by-letter (b-a-t).
2. The initial consonant is sounded, and the rest of the word is added as a word family (b-at).
3. The initial consonant with a vowel is sounded together and then the final consonant is added (ba-t).

1.12   TALKING BOOKS

Desired Outcome

The purpose of this strategy (Carbo, 1978; Chomsky, 1976) is to aid students in developing basic sight vocabulary from which phonics rules may be drawn.

General Overview

This technique uses tape-recorded books (either commercially made or recorded by the teacher), in order that the student may associate printed words with words spoken on the tape recording.

Steps Used in the Strategy

1. Cue the listener. State the page number before reading that page. Pause to allow the listener to turn the page or look at the pictures.
2. Phrase reading: emphasize clarity, expression, and logical phrasing.
3. Tactile reinforcement: instruct students to move a finger under the words as they are heard.

Additional Information

Do not use sound effects, because they will confuse listeners. This strategy is used primarily with learning-disabled children. It can be used by either classroom teachers or a reading specialist.

1.13   THEMATIC WORD WALL

Desired Outcome

This strategy (Robb, 1997) enlarges students' phonemic awareness and knowledge of letter-sound relationships and letter patterns, using words centered around a common theme.

General Overview

This strategy is both student- and teacher-directed. Once the teacher has chosen a theme, students read several books on that theme. Students select words from those books that are related to their theme. These words are used to study sound/symbol relationships, long and short vowel sounds, synonyms, and antonyms. Theme words can be listed on chart paper or on a class bulletin board for future reference.

Steps Used in the Strategy

1. Choose a theme to study (e.g., weather).
2. Have students read numerous books related to their theme.
3. Instruct students to select words from the literature that are relevant to their theme (e.g., *foggy*).
4. Next, have students record these words in boxes on a sheet of paper (or index cards) and photocopy them for the entire class.
5. Allow students to cut each word out (each will have a set of words).
6. Begin the lesson, following a procedure like this one:
   a. Ask students if they can find all the words with a particular sound/symbol relationship, such as the long vowel sound.
   b. Instruct students to sort words by the long *a, e, i, o,* and *u* sounds.

c. Have students choose one sound and then have the entire class list words that contain that sound. (For example, using *weather*, students could use the long "e" sound and list *foggy, humidity, sleet, meteorologist, flurries,* and *sunny*.)

d. Allow students to work in pairs to identify letter patterns that make a long vowel sound, such as "y" and "ee," and record them in the appropriate column. Next, instruct students to write words that contain those patterns. Add additional words when it would be helpful.

e. Reintroduce concepts from the books by having students classify related words. For example, for words connected to precipitation, group *hail, snow, rain, ice, drizzle, dew, sleet,* and *frost*.

Additional Information

These words should be left on a board (hence, Thematic Word Wall) in the room while studying a theme. The board serves as a reference to new and often complicated vocabulary. The idea is to familiarize students with words that are related and to have words easily available for the students in an understandable manner. This is an exciting way to introduce a theme and discuss the English language.

1.14   VLP (VOCABULARY, LANGUAGE, PREDICTION)

Desired Outcome

The VLP (Vocabulary, Language, Prediction) strategy (Wood & Robinson, 1983) aids students in developing their word analysis and word identification skills, which eventually leads to improved reading comprehension.

General Overview

VLP is a useful strategy that incorporates lessons on vocabulary, oral language, and prediction. Its two purposes are to provide a means for preteaching vocabulary by using oral language activities which reinforce each word's structural and semantic characteristics and to use the vocabulary as a basis for predicting what might happen in the assigned reading selection.

Steps Used in the Strategy

1. Examine the reading passage and determine important and difficult words.
2. Note the skill to be emphasized in the unit.
3. Put the words on separate flash cards.
4. Place the cards on the table in front of the students. Explain that they will see these words in the reading selection. Distribute sheets of teacher-made

FIGURE 1 in Strategy 1.13

Thematic Word Wall: Names and Characteristics of Wild Animals

lions	tigers	chimpanzees	apes	roar
fur	mane	puma	climb	trees
orangutan	herbivore	carnivore	cheetah	elephant
giraffes	zebra	gazelle	graze	hunt
koala	cougar	cobra	monkey	anteater

Long "A" Sounds	apes mane graze
Short "A" Sounds	rat carnivore anteater
Long "E" Sounds	trees cheetah zebra
Short "E" Sounds	herbivore elephant
Long "I" Sounds	lions tigers climb
Short "I" Sounds	chimpanzees giraffe
Long "O" Sounds	koala cobra orangutan roar
Short "O" Sounds	monkey
Long "U" Sounds	cougar
Short "U" Sounds	puma fur hunt

sentences, with the focus words eliminated from each sentence. Explain that the object is to fill in the blank with the word that best fits into the sentence.

5. Ask questions about the structural and conceptual elements of each word (e.g., synonyms, antonyms, categorization, homonyms, context).

6. Once they understand the vocabulary, ask students to use the words to predict what the story may be about (e.g., characterization, setting, mood/feelings, reality/fantasy, events/outcomes).

7. Record the predictions on the board for confirmation, rejection, or modification during the reading to correspond with the actual events in the reading selection.

Additional Information

VLP is a strategy that is appropriate for all learners at all ability levels. This strategy is an excellent example of a multipurpose learning aid that reinforces the necessary skills that children need in order to be successful readers. It does this by using the actual vocabulary of a selection in a meaningful context to help familiarize students with the words before reading the passage.

1.15 VOCABULARY SELF-COLLECTION

Desired Outcome

This strategy (Haggard, 1986) is designed to help students expand their vocabularies by relating their new vocabulary words to experiences that have meaning in their own lives. This exercise also allows students an opportunity for cooperative learning.

General Overview

Students are asked to use their own interests and prior experiences as the basis for learning words they encounter in reading assignments. The students work together to generate a word list from their reading. They discuss and confirm the vocabulary definitions using the context provided by reading, discussion, and the dictionary. This strategy is interactive and is based on authentic reading experiences.

Steps Used in the Strategy

1. *Select words for study.* After students have read a story or an informational text, ask them to review it and select one word for class study either as individuals, partners, or teams. In order for you to be involved in the process, also select one word for study. Encourage students to select words that seem important or interesting.

FIGURE 1 in Strategy 1.14

VLP Story: *She Did What She Wanted*

Directions: Listed below, you will find some words that will be appearing in today's reading assignment *She Did What She Wanted*. Go through this sheet and complete each section fully **before** reading this story.

I. Context. In this section, you will try to discover the meaning of the vocabulary words through context. Read the following sentences and determine which of the vocabulary words fit in the blank space.

1. The World Series determines the best _____ team in the country.
2. When you get sick, you go to a _____ to help you get better.
3. I got a speeding ticket because the police radar _____ me driving at 75 miles per hour.
4. My mom made me _____ my dog to bark when strangers come by the house.
5. I get to _____ whom I want to come to my birthday party.
6. My brother was in _____ after he got caught stealing from the store.
7. Even though I get mad very easily, I try hard to _____ my temper.
8. I like playing _____ because it doesn't hurt as much when the ball hits you.
9. If you play baseball for the Elmira Pioneers, you are a _____ baseball player.

II. Structural and Contextual Elements

Directions: From the list of vocabulary words, choose five of the words. Some of the words have more than one meaning. If you find a word that has more than one meaning, discuss both meanings and write a sentence for each separate meaning. For other words, you could substitute a different word with the same meaning. Two words that have the same meaning are called *synonyms*. Choose a synonym for one of the vocabulary words and write a sentence using the new word.

Example:
TRAIN
I am going to *train* the new person to do this job.
I am going to ride on a *train* when I go to my cousin's wedding.

DISGRACE: shame
It is a shame that some people think girls are not as smart as boys.
1.
2.
3.
4.
5.

III. Prediction

You are now very familiar with the vocabulary words from today's story. Considering these words, what do you think this story will be about? What do you think the setting is? Who do you think the characters are? What might the main plot and theme of this story be?

2. *Compile and define the words.* Ask each student or group to give the word selected for study and the definition (determined from context) of the word. List each word and the definition on the chalkboard or overhead; include your own word as well. Use the dictionary to verify or complete definitions as needed and encourage all students to participate in this process. With the students, agree on a final list of words and definitions.

3. *Finalize the word lists.* With the students, review the list to eliminate duplications, words that seem unrelated to the story or topic of study, and words that students simply do not want to study. Agree on a reasonable number (three to five) for the final list and have students put the words and definitions in their vocabulary notebooks or journals. Allow them to record words eliminated from the class list in their personal lists. When they write the words in their journals, ask them to write a sentence demonstrating the use of the word in their own lives and showing their understanding of it.

4. *Use and extend the words.* Encourage the students to use the words in their writing and to look for them in other books they read. Plan activities that reinforce the words, such as semantic maps, semantic feature analysis, and word arrays.

Additional Information

These procedures are based on the concept of vocabulary development after reading, but they can be adapted for use before reading. For prereading, the students preview the text and select for further study words that they think will be important. The Vocabulary Self-Collection strategy can be done as a prereading or postreading activity. The word lists that are generated by students can also serve as spelling lists.

1.16 WORD ANALOGIES

Desired Outcome

Word Analogies (Greenwood, 1988; Greenwood & Hoffbenkoske, 1995) can be used as preparation, assistance, or reflective reading activities. This strategy teaches critical thinking and aids in reading comprehension, vocabulary development, and connection of ideas across the curriculum.

General Overview

Word Analogies can be used with either narrative or expository text. This strategy emphasizes monitoring comprehension and vocabulary development. Word Analogies develop the skills of word analysis and comprehension.

FIGURE 1 in Strategy 1.15
Self Collection Summary

Name: _____

I. Vocabulary word selected by group:
Definition:

II. Final Word List:

III. Sentences from Final Word List:

FIGURE 2 in Strategy 1.15
Example of Vocabulary Self-Collection Strategy

Name: _____

I. Vocabulary word selected by group: excellent
   Definition: _excellent: adj., commendable, honorable,_
   extraordinary

   _____

   _____

   _____

II. Final Word List:
   excellent   election
   president   nation
   revolution

III. Sentences from Final Word List:
1. The student did an excellent job on his vocabulary worksheet, so he got an *A*.
2. Greg beat Marsha in the election for student body president.
3. The American Revolution was fought to free the colonies from Great Britain.
4. The president of the United States is the leader of our government.
5. There are 50 states in our nation.

Steps Used in the Strategy

Introducing Analogies

1. Introduce each analogy with pictures.
2. Once students are comfortable with the concept of analogies, introduce several entire analogies with one-word analogies.
3. Reverse order of simple pairs to stress the importance of sequence in analogies.

Grouping Activities

1. Use grouping activities where four words are given; students select the word that does not belong.
2. Discuss how words are classified, which word does not belong, and why.
3. Give the students groups of three words and instruct them to supply a word of their own that does belong.
4. In the final grouping activity, give the students a pair of words and have them write a sentence that tells the relationship.

Whole Analogies

1. Write three-part analogies on the board and encourage students to listen to their peers explain their thoughts about them.
2. Give students a teacher-made handout containing several incomplete analogies. Do several together and complete the rest individually.
3. Encourage students to use cooperative groups to brainstorm their own analogies and have other groups complete them.
4. Finally, have students individually create analogies, which they share.

Additional Information

Word Analogies work with students of all ability levels starting at the second grade. This strategy encourages discussion about word meanings and relationships between words.

1.17   WORD BUILDING

Desired Outcome

Word Building (Ehri & Robbins, 1992; Goswami & Mead, 1992; Gunning, 1995) is a strategic approach to teaching phonemic awareness that capitalizes on a natural tendency for students to try decoding pronounceable parts of an unknown word.

General Overview

Word Building is a strategy for teaching phonics in correlation with the natural tendency of students to seek out pronounceable word parts. This technique can be used as a prereading activity for learning to decode new words as well as a during reading activity, as it involves reading, writing, listening, and speaking. It includes techniques for teaching phonic elements and strategies students can use to decode difficult words. The idea behind Word Building is to build on that which students already know. It is a teacher-directed activity to be used with beginning readers and students with decoding difficulties. By using this strategy, students develop a phonetic approach to decoding which helps increase their fluency, leading to better literacy comprehension.

Steps Used in the Strategy

1. Introduce a word pattern to students, such as "at." Write it on the board and have several students read it. Ask students what letter should be added to "at" to form the word *sat*. As you add the "s" to "at," enunciate the "s" and the "at" and then the whole word. Then have students read the word. Write "at" underneath *sat* (letters lined up) and ask students what letter should be added to "at" to make *hat*. Use this procedure and continue making words, such as *mat, fat, rat, cat,* and *that*. Have students note that all the words end with the letters "at." Call attention to the individual letter sounds.
2. Guided practice: provide a variety of opportunities for children to practice using the pattern being studied. Some possibilities include shared reading of big books and use of magnetic blocks.
3. Application: provide ample opportunities for students to read whole stories, books, and poems that incorporate the word pattern.

Additional Information

This strategy works for Readiness Kindergarten-First grade. This strategy can be taught to beginning readers who are starting to learn to decode words or to students who are having difficulty detecting certain sounds in a word.

1.18 WORD CLUSTER

Desired Outcome

The purpose of the Word Cluster strategy (Higginson & Phelan, 1986) is to develop students' vocabularies and their organizational skills by actively interacting with the words to be learned. This active organization and interaction gives meaning and purpose to the exercise.

FIGURE 1 in Strategy 1.17
Word Building Using-air Words

Directions: Fill in the blank with the letter or letters needed to form the correct word.

Words to choose from: hair, pair, fair, stair

On your head, you have __air.

You need *both* socks to have a __air.

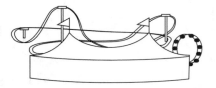
You go on rides and see strange things at the county __air.

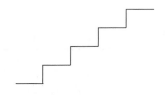
To go from one floor to another, you climb the __air.

General Overview

Word Cluster is a strategy for vocabulary development which is based on interaction with other learners as vocabulary resources. Students cluster similar words into a hierarchy. Doing so enhances their understanding of the subtle differences among words having similar meanings. Classification and association are integral parts in the Word Cluster strategy.

Steps Used in the Strategy

1. Prior to beginning the lesson, identify the word or phrase that is central to the theme or purpose of the lesson.
2. Write the name or phrase on the chalkboard and ask students to name other words having meanings similar to that of the word or phrase.
3. Record all responses on the board in the order generated by students. Try to obtain up to 15 responses.
4. When the desired number of responses has been obtained, ask students to organize the words into a cluster, or group, that can be justified. A cluster is defined as a "small, close group." Organize the cluster into a hierarchy to reflect word relationships.

EXAMPLE: A SOCIAL STUDIES TOPIC: TOWN

Initial Cluster	Hierarchy
town	neighborhood
village	community
community	village
city	town
metropolis	city
neighborhood	metropolis
megalopolis	megalopolis

Additional Information

The Word Cluster instructional strategy requires very little preparation time for the teacher but should always relate to the lesson at hand. When used as a prereading strategy, it can generate interest in a story, a poem, an article, or a study topic, while also tapping students' prior knowledge of a subject. When used as a postreading strategy, Word Cluster acts as a means of assessing student understanding of the organization of a particular concept. Word Cluster enhances students' ability to identify words appropriate in a given context and to choose the most effective word.

FIGURE 1 in Strategy 1.18
Word Cluster: Education

Brainstorming List

elementary school

nursery school

high school

middle school

university

medical school

graduate school

vocational school

junior college

community college

Hierarchy

nursery school

elementary school

middle school

high school

junior college

vocational school

community college

university

graduate school

medical school

1.19   WORD EXPANSIONS

Desired Outcome

This strategy (Floriani, 1989) helps children improve their word attack skills. It specifically enables students to use sight words to develop phonemic awareness and structural analysis.

General Overview

Basic sight words are repeatedly presented to the reader in a variety of contexts. This enables the students to apply what they have learned and helps them develop confidence by being successful.

Steps Used in the Strategy

1. Write a sight word on one side of a card and a sentence using the word on the other.
2. After adding 6 to 10 words to the students' word bank, review and practice them, so that the students can identify them instantly. Have the students expand on the words by adding inflectional endings, suffixes, and prefixes. Write each new word on a separate card.
3. Provide the reader with paraphrased sentences where the syntax has been altered, so that the student can use the word in different syntactic contexts.

Additional Information

The students need to experience variations of the sample root word in conjunction with syntactic, semantic, and graphophonic contexts. Samples of words that could be used in this strategy follow:

like	likeness	likely
fun	funny	funnier
friend	friendly	friendliest

1.20   WORD SORT

Desired Outcome

The purpose of this strategy (Johnson & Lehnert, 1984) is to teach students phonics by having the student verbally sort known words into categories. This technique will also build sight word vocabulary.

General Overview

In this strategy, word cards are used to promote the teaching of phonics and word identification by using a sound/symbol relationship. It works best for students who have trouble with phonics and are beginning readers.

Steps Used in the Strategy

1. Prepare word cards from chosen vocabulary/sight words.
2. Next, prepare category cards, using categories into which the chosen words will fit.

   Example words: *dress, dressed, dressing;* categories: past, present, and future

3. Model the procedure by orally identifying a word and placing it into the appropriate category.
4. Encourage students to pronounce the words themselves and place them in the correct categories.
5. When the students can complete the entire task without prompting, prepare a new set of cards.

Additional Information

This strategy can be a game. It can be timed so that the students learn to recognize words immediately and the sound symbol pattern becomes a part of their sight vocabulary. If the strategy is used in a group, the teacher can pass out several cards to each student.

1.21   WORD STORM

Desired Outcome

Students using this strategy (Klemp, 1994) improve vocabulary skills. This strategy focuses on reading, writing, listening, and speaking skills. These are techniques which aid in increasing vocabulary analysis and vocabulary comprehension skills.

General Overview

Word Storm incorporates the use of vocabulary words in context with the students' understanding of the meaning of the words. Students are guided through an in-depth analysis of a vocabulary word, its synonyms, and its applications. It is essentially a brain "storming" technique; students "storm" about particular words—their meaning, usage, and so on. This strategy may be used as a preteaching, prereading activity for upper elementary grades through the secondary grades and is best used by students who work well in small groups. Word Storm may be beneficial when addressing content area subjects.

Steps Used in the Strategy

1. Give students a Word Storm sheet containing questions that pertain to the word assigned. Questions on this sheet might include the following:

   What is the word?
   Write the sentence from the text in which the word is used.
   What are some words that you think of when you hear this word?
   What are some different forms of the word?
   Name three people who would be most likely to use the word besides teachers.
   What are some other ways of saying the same thing?
   Make up a sentence using this word.
   Let your sentence tell what the word means.

2. Divide the class into very small groups or pairs and assign each group a word to study.
3. Instruct each group to respond to each of the questions on its activity sheet.
4. Allow students to use a dictionary, thesaurus, glossary, and so on to answer their questions, thereby promoting dictionary and research skills.
5. Next, have students share their words with other groups by stating and defining their words, using their Word Storm sheets as a guide.

Additional Information

When more than one group has the same word, there might be additional insights into the use of the word. When the activity is used in pairs, a situation is created in which students are teaching each other the words. This activity could be used when the teacher has numerous vocabulary words to introduce. It can be used in correlation with dictionary and research skills. Also each group could act out its word in a skit.

FIGURE 1 in Strategy 1.21
Word Storm

Name: _____   Word: _____

Write the sentence in which the word is used in the text.

What are some words you think of when you hear this word?

What are some different forms of the word?

Name three people who would be most likely to use this word, besides teachers.

What are some other ways of saying the same thing?

Make up a sentence using this word—make sure your sentence makes it clear what the word means.

Chapter
2

Meaning Vocabulary Strategies

2.1 ADJECTIVE/VERB/NOUN WORD MAPS

Desired Outcome

This strategy (Banwart & Duffelmeyer, 1993; Hansen & Pearson, 1983; Schwartz & Raphael, 1985) visually represents words and can be used with nouns, verbs, and adjectives to expand students' word meanings.

General Overview

A Noun Word Map focuses on a target concept, which may be a word or phrase that answers the question, What is it? The map emphasizes several salient characteristics of the target word, as well as gives examples. An Adjective Word Map focuses on what the adjective describes and what it means (synonyms). It also gives some examples. The Verb Word Maps are most effective for words that reflect an overt action or movement. The Verb Word Map focuses on what the verb describes and examples of situations where the verb would be applicable.

Steps Used in the Strategy

Noun Word Map

1. Place the noun in the center square of the word map. Have students fill in the square above the noun, telling what it is.
2. Next, have students fill in the spaces beside the noun, using descriptive words or adjectives that describe the noun.
3. Finally, have students fill in the spaces below the target word with some examples.

Adjective Word Map

1. Place the adjective (adj.) in the center square of the word map. Have students fill in the square(s) above the adjective, telling what the word describes.
2. Next, have students fill in the spaces beside the adjective, using words that tell what the adjective means.
3. Finally, fill in the spaces below the adjective to give some examples of what the adjective means.

Verb Word Map

1. Place the verb in the center square of the word map. Have students fill in the square(s) above the verb, telling what the word describes.
2. Next, fill in the spaces beside the verb, using words that give examples of situations that clarify the meaning of the verb.
3. Finally, fill in the spaces below the verb to give some examples of what the verb means.

Additional Information

This strategy can be used at all grade levels and with any type of reading program. When used in kindergarten and first grade, pictures and drawings can be used in place of words.

2.2   BIG BOOKS

Desired Outcome

The desired outcomes of this strategy (Crowley, 1991) are to build children's confidence in reading and to promote participation in a large group.

General Overview

The use of Big Books (shared reading) enables children to read in a risk-free environment of their peers. It focuses on meaning, print, and prediction. Big Books can be used at any time. A Big Book is especially useful when there are several small duplicates. The students can use them during free time to read silently or to a friend. Big Books promote confidence and enthusiasm in a language-first approach.

Steps Used in the Strategy

1. Choose a Big Book and read it aloud to the students several times. Make sure to introduce the book title, author, and illustrator. Ask the students to predict the events in the book.
2. After the children are familiar with the story line and words, read the story together with the students as a class.
3. Have a discussion before reading, during reading, and/or after reading the Big Book. Through discussion, focus on vocabulary, comprehension, sequencing or any other aspect of the story.
4. Provide follow-up activities to reinforce learning. For example: A Big Book with a lot of "short ă" words could be used as a base to teach the "short ă" sound.

Additional Information

Readiness Kindergarten-Second Grade are good age levels for this strategy. Big Books are effective with beginner and emergent students. It is also useful for shy students, because they all participate in shared reading. They all read together at the same time.

FIGURE 1 in Strategy 2.1
Verb Word Map

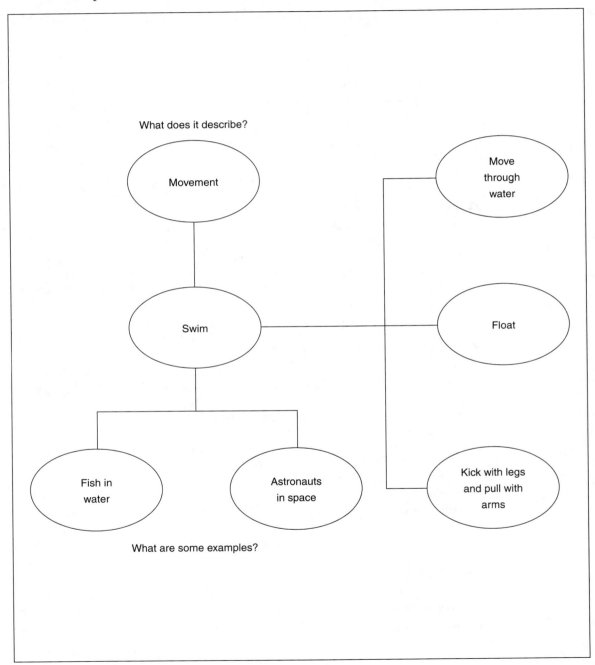

FIGURE 2 in Strategy 2.1
Verb Word Map

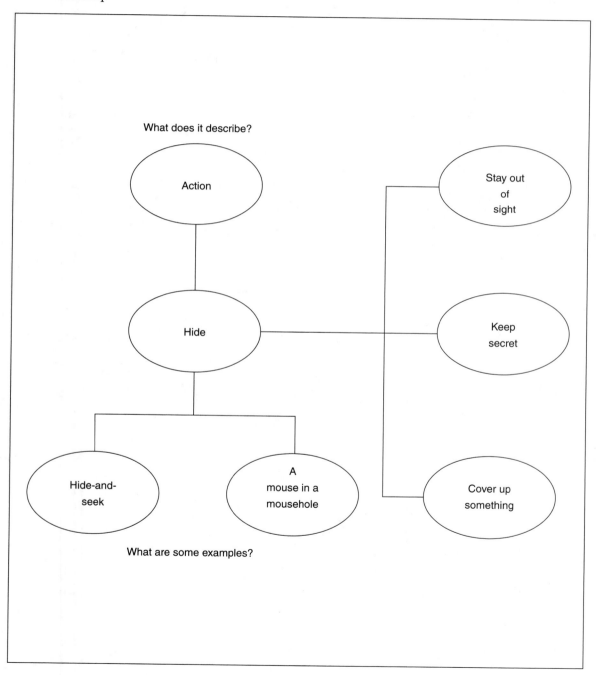

FIGURE 3 in Strategy 2.1
Adjective Word Map

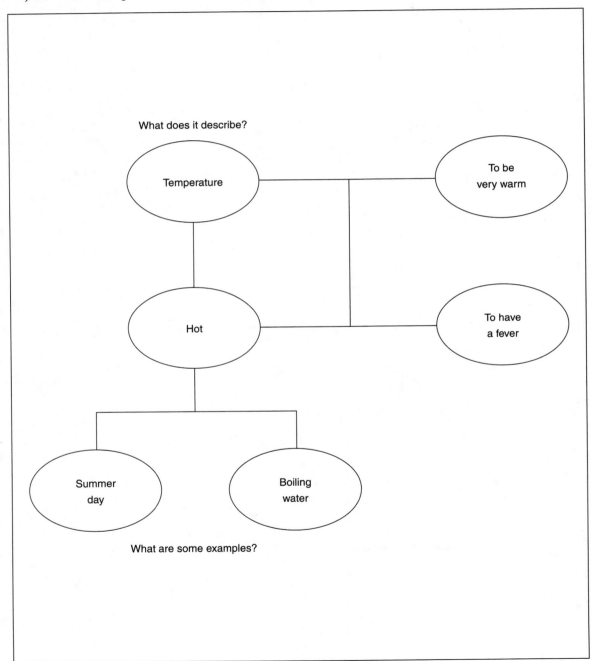

2.3   CAPSULES

Desired Outcome

The desired outcome of this strategy (Crist, 1975; Flatley & Rutland, 1986) is to increase vocabulary base knowledge and vocabulary-building skills, helping students relate new vocabulary words to specific topics and categories.

General Overview

Each Capsule contains important vocabulary words relating to a particular topic. Such Capsule titles could include food, family, or sports—anything of interest to the students. Students are instructed to listen, speak, read, and write the words, providing more exposure to each term. Capsules are effective with both narrative and expository texts and can be used at any grade level.

Steps Used in the Strategy

1. *Prepare a Capsule.* Review the text, extracting key words that the student should learn. You can vary the number of words in the Capsule, depending on the grade level of the students.
2. *Introduce the Capsule.* Have a 5- to 15-minute discussion with the students about the text that was just reviewed. During the conversation, use the new vocabulary and have the students attempt to identify the words. As you expose each word, write and discuss it.
3. *Reinforce speaking vocabulary.* To automatize the new vocabulary and reinforce speaking skills, place students into small groups to discuss the Capsule words for another 5–10 minutes. Have students use as many words as possible.
4. *Reinforce writing vocabulary.* Encourage students to write short paragraphs or stories using as many of the new words as possible.

Additional Information

This strategy is also effective with linguistically and culturally different students. The students use their prior knowledge to express their interpretation of the story while using new reading skills and vocabulary terms. Each week a new Capsule should be introduced, discussed, and worked on. The old Capsule lists should be placed in a classroom area visible to students.

2.4   CLOZE INSTRUCTION

Desired Outcome

Students are able to increase their sentence comprehension and word meaning skills through practicing this word deletion strategy (Carr, Dewitz, & Patberg, 1989).

General Overview

The Cloze Instruction technique develops comprehension by deleting target words from a text. This encourages the student to think about what word would make sense in the sentence and in the context of the entire story.

Steps Used in the Strategy

1. Select a text of 200–400 words.
2. Decide on target words within the text.
3. Systematically delete the words from a paragraph and insert a blank for each deleted word.
4. Instruct students to read the whole passage in order to get a sense of the entire meaning.
5. Encourage students to fill in the blanks in the passage.
6. When students are finished filling in the blanks, evaluate the answers as to the similarity of meaning between the deleted word and the supplied word.
7. Allow students to review and talk about what strategies they used to make their word choices.

Additional Information

This technique is targeted for reading levels 4–12. The text to be chosen for this instruction should be paragraphs and stories that are coherent. This technique can also be done orally to develop predictive listening in young children. This strategy facilitates comprehension in students who have verbal fluency by encouraging the combination of text and meaning cues.

2.5   CONCEPTUAL MAPPING

Desired Outcome

Students practicing this strategy (Flood & Lapp, 1988; Taylor & Beach, 1984) develop organizational and comprehension skills and an understanding of the relationships between key elements of given text.

FIGURE 1 in Strategy 2.4
Cloze Instruction

Directions: Read the passage below. You will notice that several words are missing and have been replaced with blanks. From the context of the sentence, decide on the correct word and place it in the blank.
Hint The words are from this week's spelling list.

Jennifer and Karen are _____. They like to go to the _____ because they enjoy playing in the sand and waves. They like to play in the sand and create sand _____. One day they spent _____ creating an entire village from the _____. The village contained stores and _____. They also made _____ out of _____ to park on the streets. After working all day, they were reluctant to leave it and go home. They were _____ the tide would _____ it. The next day they returned and saw that their _____ was safe.

General Overview

Conceptual maps are graphic organizers that aid learners. The use of mapping works for all students but especially for those with poor organizational skills, those who have difficulty making connections between points, those who focus too much on details and miss main points, and those who find visual cues helpful. Examples of conceptual maps include charts, graphs, illustrations, and flow charts. They can be used with any grade level with both narrative and expository texts.

Steps Used in the Strategy

1. Prepare the students by having them brainstorm any background knowledge they may already have about the subject.
2. Depending on the knowledge and skill levels of the students, determine whether to use a blank map or a partially completed map. With extremely disabled readers, use explicit directives such as arrows, color codes, and shape codes.
3. Explain the organized structure of the map and its usefulness to the text. Also explain the importance of using the maps for studying.
4. Ask the students to complete the map with you. Work on the map section by section as you read.
5. After the map has been completed, ask the students to use it for studying or as notes for an extended reading, writing, or oral assignment.
6. Display the map on a wall in the classroom for future references.

Additional Information

Conceptual maps are excellent visual aids. They are versatile and can be used as a prereading, during reading, or postreading guide. They can also be used as study guides or as part of a unit wrap-up. It is possible to make many modifications for mapping. Students can make their own maps or create a class map. Unit maps can be made as an introductory lesson, and specific maps can be made for smaller topics.

2.6 CONTEXTUAL PROCESSING

Desired Outcome

The purpose of this strategy (Tipton, 1991) is to help students develop the skills needed to determine word meanings through contextual clues.

General Overview

Contextual processing is a technique used to develop new word meanings as they are found in the context of a selected story. This technique shows the student how to use context to figure out the meaning of new vocabulary words.

FIGURE 1 in Strategy 2.5
Sequential Graphic Organizer for Humpty-Dumpty

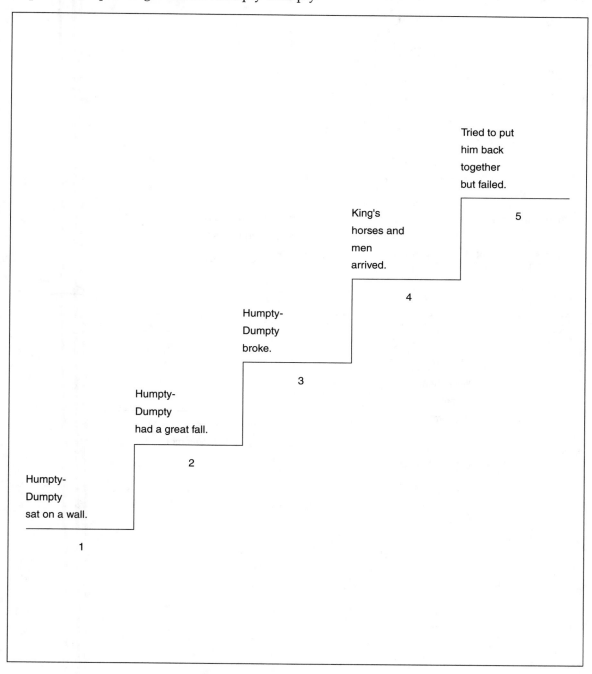

FIGURE 2 in Strategy 2.5
Graphic Organizer: Cause and Effect—the Water Cycle

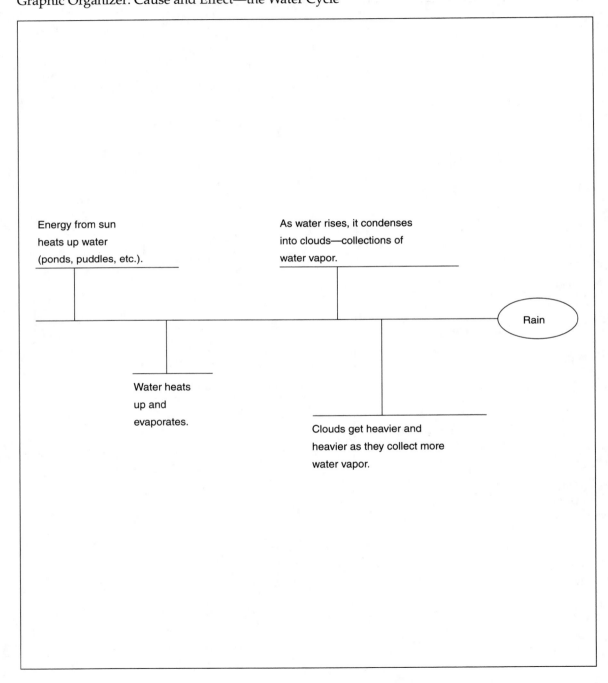

FIGURE 3 in Strategy 2.5
Graphic Organizer: Problem and Solution

Cinderella

Prince Charming wants to find the beautiful woman from the ball.	He tries her slipper on the foot of every woman in the kingdom.	He finds Cinderella; they get married and live happily ever after.

Steps Used in the Strategy

1. Select unfamiliar key vocabulary words to teach.
2. Find a passage in the text where the meaning of the word is apparent when using the surrounding context. If a passage is not available, create your own three-sentence paragraph.
3. Write the paragraph on the overhead or chalkboard.
4. Read the paragraph aloud to students.
5. Have the students reread the paragraph silently.
6. Ask the students about the meaning of the word found in the paragraph—for example, "What does the paragraph tell you about the word?"
7. Use student answers to probe for further understanding by asking, "Why did you think that?"
8. Ask the students to write down what the new word might mean.
9. Have the students think of other, similar situations in which they might use the word.
10. Have students think of other words with similar meanings.
11. Have students record target words and a personal definition in their notebooks.

Additional Information

This strategy is used with paragraphs, three or four sentences long, in which the meaning of the new vocabulary is apparent from the surrounding context. Contextual Processing has students figure out unfamiliar word meanings from the context.

2.7 CONTEXTUAL REDEFINITION

Desired Outcome

The desired outcome of this strategy (Cunningham, Cunningham, & Arthur, 1981) is to help students use context to unlock the meanings of unknown words and to make informed, rather than haphazard, guesses about word meanings, using context as clues.

General Overview

This strategy stresses the importance of context in predicting and verifying word meanings. It involves reading, writing, and verifying the definition of the word in context and then in the dictionary. It is easy to implement and requires little teacher preparation. The student is actively involved in learning the definition, rather than merely being told it.

Steps Used in the Strategy

1. *Select unfamiliar words.* Choose words related to the reading assignment that students will need to know in order to understand the text material.
2. *Write a sentence.* If the word is used in the context of material being read, use the sentence the author used. If not, provide the students with one.
3. *Present words in isolation.* Using an overhead transparency or a chalkboard, ask students to provide definitions for each word. Pronounce each word as it is introduced. Write these definitions on the overhead or chalkboard to be checked later.
4. *Present the words in context.* Present the students with the sentences you wrote earlier. Again, ask students to come up with a definition.
5. *Use a dictionary for verification.* Ask students to consult a dictionary to verify the guesses offered. Share the dictionary definition with the class. Discuss the quality of predictions given when the words are presented (a) in isolation and (b) in context.

Additional Information

This strategy is used to teach new vocabulary, not to reinforce vocabulary words. Teachers must provide extensive activities for reinforcement.

2.8   ELVES (EXCITE, LISTEN, VISUALIZE, EXTEND, AND SAVOR)

Desired Outcome

ELVES (Levesque, 1989) stands for Excite, Listen, Visualize, Extend, and Savor. It is a strategy designed to develop listening comprehension and maintain children's initial excitement about reading.

General Overview

This strategy focuses on building skills while exciting children about reading. It can also be used by parents at bedtime or by teachers during class for a wide variety of stories.

Steps Used in the Strategy

1. *Excite.* Begin reading aloud, with a discussion, by focusing on the listener's personal experiences related to the theme, character, or plot of the story.
2. *Listen.* In order to facilitate listening comprehension, develop an environment where the listener, message, and listening situation interact.

Direct students to predict what will happen in the story and encourage them to remember exactly when their prediction was rejected or confirmed.

3. *Visualize.* Use guided mental imagery as a powerful strategy for teaching children to generate meaning. Practice oral language and assess comprehension by encouraging them to verbalize their imagery.

4. *Extend.* Encourage listeners to achieve higher levels of meaning by bridging knowledge stored within their own minds with new information found in the story. Facilitate listening comprehension by asking questions that put listeners in the role of active meaning makers.

5. *Savor.* Encourage students to savor and slowly digest the story. Give listeners time to reflect on the good thoughts and feelings the story stimulated. Include activities which allow the listeners to build on the meaning made during the listening experience.

Additional Information
This may help students who have trouble with listening comprehension.

2.9   GRIP (GENERATIVE RECIPROCAL INSTRUCTIONAL PROCEDURE)

Desired Outcome
This strategy (Reutzel & Hollingsworth, 1988) is designed to help students attend effectively to text clues to make inferences in reading.

General Overview
GRIP (Generative Reciprocal Instructional Procedure) was designed to provide an effective delivery system for vocabulary and comprehension instruction.

Steps Used in the Strategy
1. Highlight key vocabulary in a passage.
2. Generate lists of clue words.
3. Write short inferential passages.
4. Give students the opportunity to decipher the meaning of the vocabulary.
5. Encourage students to create their own GRIP passages, giving other students the opportunity to solve them.

Additional Information
This strategy helps children identify key vocabulary in text, generate their own vocabulary lists and passages, transfer this knowledge to the solution of inferential

passages created by others, and apply these skills to making inferences in unfamiliar materials.

2.10 KEYWORDS

Desired Outcome

The Keywords method (Konopak & Williams, 1988) is a study strategy for all-ability-level readers that includes using familiar, concrete images to aid in learning difficult information.

General Overview

The Keywords method requires the student to associate new information with a familiar image to aid in later recall. It uses a process which involves recoding, relating, and retrieving. *Recoding* occurs when the student transforms the unfamiliar word into a keyword that looks or sounds like the original. The student then *relates* the new word to the keyword through the use of an interactive image. The student then uses the keyword to *retrieve* the correct meaning when encountering the new word.

Steps Used in the Strategy

Guidelines for Introducing the Strategy
1. Select important facts to be learned (e.g., names of minerals and their uses).
2. Pair each fact with a keyword you have identified (e.g., *appetite-apple*-use in industry).
3. Create a picture, with the keyword interacting with the new fact (e.g., an apple sitting on a workbench in a factory).
4. Develop a drawing of this picture or construct a visual statement describing the picture.

General Guidelines for Instruction
5. Explain the Keywords method to students.
6. Model the procedure, using examples from information that is to be learned.
7. Walk students through the procedure, using practice exercises involving the new material.
8. Provide additional exercises they can work on independently and discuss afterwards.
9. Give specific instruction on when to use such a method for different learning tasks.

Additional Information

This strategy can be used with young readers as well as with those reading at the most advanced levels. The Keywords method is a study skill that can be used with readers of varying ability levels.

2.11   LIST-GROUP-LABEL (LGL)

Desired Outcome

The goals of this strategy (Anderson & Barnitz, 1984; Wood & Mateja, 1983) are to help students improve their vocabulary and categorization skills, to teach students to organize verbal concepts, and to reinforce new vocabulary terms.

General Overview

One of the ways students develop the concepts for words is to learn how their meanings interrelate. List-Group-Label (LGL) is a classification strategy that helps students learn how words relate to previously learned concepts. In essence, LGL attempts to improve on the way in which students learn and remember new concepts.

Steps Used in the Strategy

1. Select a one- or two-word topic for study. Make sure there are several subtopics for the topic you have chosen. Select the topic from a subject area, an upcoming reading, a theme students are studying, a holiday, and so on.
2. Write the name of the topic on the chalkboard or overhead transparency. Ask students to think of all the terms that are associated with the topic. Have students work in groups or as a class to brainstorm words related to the topic. Use 15–25 words. List words on the chalkboard and add ones that are missing. Use words that are familiar to students. If a suggestion is made that is unfamiliar, ask the student to define the word in relation to the topic.
3. Read the list orally and point to each word. Then ask students to organize the list into smaller groups and to give each group a label. Have students work in small groups or alone. Be prepared for a variety of answers. Place words into groups. Because the object of the lesson is for students to interact with the concepts, you can allow them to differ on some decisions about where an item would fit in a list. Place some terms under more than one label.
4. Encourage students to add words to the categories on the organized lists. Impose a meaningful organization on a list of concepts, so students can find that related concepts can be more easily recalled from memory.
5. If students are working in groups, have each group share with the entire class its method of characterization and the words that group members chose to add. List the categories and labels on the chalkboard or a transparency.

Encourage lively discussions as students analyze words and concepts for shared and defining features.

6. Have students extend the strategy by transforming their list into a semantic web.

Additional Information

This strategy can be modified to fit any need. Younger students can work in groups to categorize and find the relationship among the vocabulary words. The responses should be displayed in a reasonable place for future reference. Students should have some prior knowledge of the topic to be discussed in order for the strategy to work. List-Group-Label can be used with students at all grade levels. A beneficial aspect of List-Group-Label that should be emphasized is the sharing and modeling of thought processes. This may result in students' expanding their experiential background and changing their view of a concept. LGL is a valuable diagnostic tool. In a prereading situation, the teacher can find out what it is that students know and what it is that will require teacher instruction. In a postreading situation, teachers can determine what students have learned and what will require reteaching. As a vocabulary development lesson, teachers can develop a source of words from students' experiences that might need clarification.

2.12 LITERATURE CIRCLES

Desired Outcome

The goal of this strategy is to increase students' higher-level comprehension by helping students develop a comfortable, personal response to literature.

General Overview

Literature Circles are used to develop personal responses to literature by having students share their interpretations in a discussion group. This allows the students to integrate the author's ideas with their own. The targeted reading levels are K–12.

Steps Used in the Strategy

1. Introduce several books by giving short summaries of them.
2. Instruct students to choose a book to read for the next two days/week.
3. After books have been read, have additional students read the same books and gather into a Literature Circle.
4. Begin an open-ended discussion with an invitation such as, "Tell me about the book," or "What was your favorite part?"
5. At the end of discussion time, allow the group to decide on a topic to discuss the following day.

FIGURE 1 in Strategy 2.11
List-Group-Label

Topic: Democracy

Word List:

USA	Constitution	Voting
President	Canada	Trial by Jury
England	Freedom of Speech	Congress Members
The People	Senate	Legislature
Freedom	Freedom of the Press	Laws

Group:

Group 1: USA
Canada
England

Group 2: Freedom of Speech
Freedom
Freedom of the Press
Voting
Trial by Jury
Laws

Group 3: Constitution
Senate
Legislature

Group 4: President
Congress Members
The People

Label:

Group 1: Countries that have democracies
Group 2: Rights protected by democracies
Group 3: Institutions within democracies
Group 4: The people who have power within a democracy

6. As time goes on, become less involved in the discussion.
7. When the students are finished with the discussion, have the group present their interpretations to the class as a "book talk."

Additional Information

This technique is appropriate for students who can discuss their ideas freely in a group. The dialogue helps students elaborate their understanding of literature and connect that understanding to their own experiences. A writing component can also be added, so that students can share their ideas more easily.

2.13 MARGINAL GLOSSES

Desired Outcome

The goal of this strategy (Stewart & Cross, 1991) is to improve student comprehension of text material and vocabulary.

General Overview

Marginal Glosses is a reading strategy that provides an interrelationship among the reader, author, and teacher to promote active participation. This strategy helps relate prior learning to new information gathered from the text.

Steps Used in the Strategy

1. Choose an excerpt from the text to be read and decide on vocabulary or concepts that need to be learned.
2. Make a photocopy of the material. In the margins, write statements, questions, or vocabulary definitions next to the appropriate paragraph as an elaboration of the information.
3. Direct students to read Marginal Glosses as they read the material. This gives students definitions of vocabulary words or more background information related to prior learning.
4. After reading, promote a discussion of the material.

Additional Information

This strategy is geared toward upper elementary and high school students. It requires preparation time but provides a lot of additional information.

2.14   MOTOR IMAGING

Desired Outcome

The desired outcome of this strategy (Casale, 1985) is to increase vocabulary comprehension.

General Overview

Motor Imaging procedures encourage students to connect a new word with a pantomime or psychomotor meaning, as well as a language meaning. The language meaning of the word is given immediately in Step 1 and is translated to a motor meaning and reinforced in subsequent steps.

Steps Used in the Strategy

1. Write the word on the chalkboard, pronounce it, and define it.
2. Ask students to imagine a simple pantomime for the word meaning (how could you show someone what this word means?).
3. Instruct students that, when you give a specific signal, they are to do pantomimes simultaneously.
4. Select the most common pantomime form observed. Show the pantomime to students, who then say the word while doing the pantomime.
5. Repeat each new word, directing the class to do the pantomime and to say a brief meaning or synonym.
6. Direct students to read a selection containing the new words.

Additional Information

The consistency of students' pantomimes for a given new word meaning suggests that fairly common psychomotor meanings exist and are effectively elicited and elaborated. Motor Imaging is most appropriate for the less verbal students, who rely on their experiences when interpreting texts. By pantomiming and acting out the meanings of the words, they can relate their experiences to verbal information. In order for this technique to work well, the students need to be able to act out images and relate the action to the word meaning.

2.15   POSSIBLE SENTENCES

Desired Outcome

Students practicing this strategy (Kapinus & Stahl, 1991) use predictions and idea generation to expand their vocabulary base and improve their skills for learning and comprehending new vocabulary words.

General Overview

Possible Sentences was designed to help students determine the meanings and relationships of new vocabulary words. Students make predictions about the unknown words, then read to verify and/or refine their predictions. Prediction is used to create interest and to focus the students' attention on the meanings and concepts to be acquired. This strategy can be used with middle and secondary students in the content areas. However, it can be modified to suit all levels of expository text.

Steps Used in the Strategy

1. *List key vocabulary.* Predetermine the words that are essential to the reading and list the vocabulary on the board. It is important that you also pronounce the words for the students while listing them.
2. *Elicit sentences.* Ask students to use at least two words from the list in a sentence (one they think could be in the text). Record the sentences on the board and underline the vocabulary words. Encourage the students to use every word from the list at least once. Continue until they cannot produce any more sentences.
3. *Read and verify sentences.* Ask students to read the text to check the accuracy of the sentences generated.
4. *Evaluate sentences.* Follow with a discussion to evaluate each prediction sentence. Omit or revise sentences that are not accurate.
5. *Generate new sentences.* After the original sentences have been evaluated and revised, ask for additional sentences. As new sentences are given, check them for accuracy and have the students record them in their notebooks.

Additional Information

It is important to choose vocabulary words that can be defined by the context of the reading passage, as well as to use some words that may be familiar to students already. This strategy can work for students with either a great deal or very little prior knowledge. Students who otherwise may not participate if they know they have to give the "right" answer might participate in this activity. This also gives students who are unmotivated a purpose for reading. This strategy also allows the teacher to assess the students' vocabulary knowledge before reading the text.

2.16   PREDICT-O-GRAM

Desired Outcome

Predict-O-Gram (Blachowicz, 1986) is a prereading activity which helps increase students' understanding of vocabulary terms.

General Overview

Students predict how words will be related to specific concepts in their reading selection. Predicting the uses of vocabulary words aids in story comprehension. Prior to reading, students fill in the Predict-O-Gram chart with words from a teacher-generated list. The words may be related to setting, plot, characters, problems or goals, action, resolution and other aspects of the upcoming reading selection. Following reading, students compare their chart or the class chart with the text. Students may move words to their proper places in the chart if necessary.

Steps Used in the Strategy

Teacher Preparation

1. On selection of the material, scan it to find words that will fit into these categories: setting, characters, goal or problem, action, resolution, and other topics.
2. Decide if the class is going to complete the Predict-O-Gram chart as a whole group, independently, or with a partner.
3. Scramble the order of the words and give the students the list.
4. Provide a Predict-O-Gram chart for each student.

Strategy Steps

1. Review and discuss the following terms: *setting, characters, goal or problem, action, resolution,* and *other topics.*
2. Provide the word list.
3. Have students complete the Predict-O-Gram independently, in pairs, in small groups, or as a whole class.
4. Read the selected text to students or have them read the material silently.
5. Instruct students to return to the Predict-O-Gram and check predictions or word meanings, or change words that were misplaced. Have students substantiate their reasons for their selections.

Additional Information

Students can write the vocabulary words on Post-It Notes. These can be easily moved if misplaced. The teacher should limit the number of words to 10–20.

2.17 PYRAMID

Desired Outcome

The desired outcome of this strategy (Flatley & Rutland, 1986; Levenson, 1979) is to reinforce vocabulary terms and comprehension of the text, including vocabulary and major concepts.

FIGURE 1 in Strategy 2.16
Predict-O-Gram

Directions: What do you think these words will be used to tell about? Write them on a square on the Predict-O-Gram. You may have more than one word on a square.

Slipper	Curfew	Magic
Prince	Mice	Pumpkin
Blonde	Unhappy	Running
Step-sisters	Beautiful	Drudge
Fairy Godmother	Beautiful	Discovery
Dancing	Ball	Wand
	Wedding	

Predict-O-Gram for: <u>Cinderella</u>

Setting	Characters	Goal or Problem
Action	**Resolution**	**Other Topics**

General Overview

The Pyramid is a postreading strategy that guides students through the process of finding the main idea as it develops in the text. It organizes information according to details, middle-level ideas, main ideas, and topics. Pyramiding promotes interaction as students search, discuss, arrange, categorize, and label ideas.

Steps Used in the Strategy

1. Instruct students to read the assigned text.
2. As students state facts from the text, write them on large index cards or sentence strips.
3. Display the cards in random order.
4. Instruct students to sort the cards into groups and arrange the groups in one horizontal line. Have this line form the base of the Pyramid.
5. Draw in the next tier of the Pyramid and solicit labels for the groups on the baseline. Form the second tier of the Pyramid with these labels.
6. Draw the third tier but leave it blank. Skip to the very top of the Pyramid. Ask the students what the text is about. Write the subject in one or two words in the top block of the Pyramid.
7. Encourage students to agree on a complete sentence that includes all of the information in the Pyramid so far. Derive the statement by asking what the author is saying about the subject. Put the statement into the vacant tier.

2.18   SEMANTIC FEATURE ANALYSIS

Desired Outcome

The goals of this strategy (Anders & Bos, 1986) are to improve students' vocabulary, to help students understand familiarities and differences among different concepts, and to improve students' categorization skills.

General Overview

Semantic Feature Analysis is a grid-like formation used to organize topics that have overlapping characteristics. It is a systematic organization for categorizing. Topics that are similar and different are explored, and common features are discovered. Using Semantic Feature Analysis helps students realize that several words may have certain features in common. It also helps them learn the distinguishing concepts behind words.

FIGURE 1 in Strategy 2.17

Example of a Pyramid for *Anne of Green Gables*

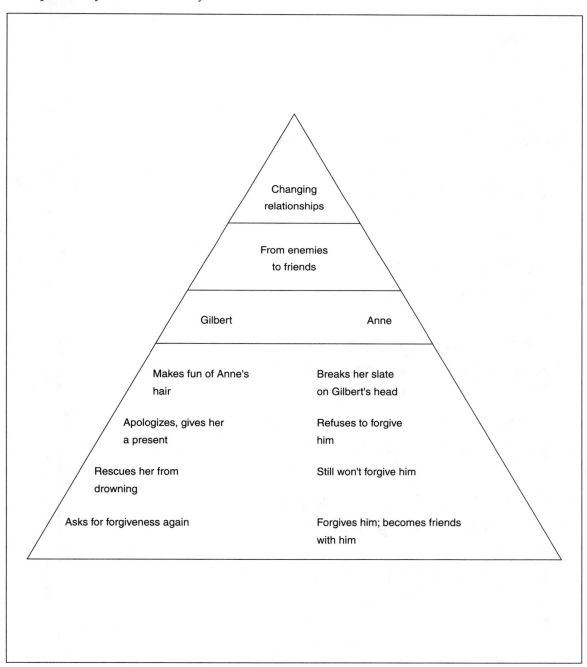

FIGURE 2 in Strategy 2.17
Example of a Story Pyramid for *Curious George and the Dump Truck*

1. <u>George</u>
Name of Main Character

2. <u>curious</u> <u>naughty</u>
Two Words Main Characters

3. <u>outside</u> <u>construction</u> <u>noisy</u>
Three Words Describing Setting

4. <u>George</u> <u>dumped</u> <u>the</u> <u>sand</u>
Four Words Stating Problem

5. <u>the</u> <u>police</u> <u>siren</u> <u>scared</u> <u>George</u>
Five Words Describing One Event

6. <u>George</u> <u>ran</u> <u>up</u> <u>the</u> <u>telephone</u> <u>pole</u>
Six Words Describing Second Event

7. <u>George</u> <u>came</u> <u>out</u> <u>of</u> <u>his</u> <u>hiding</u> <u>place</u>
Seven Words Describing Third Event

8. <u>Curious</u> <u>dumped</u> <u>sand</u> <u>and</u> <u>caught</u> <u>the</u> <u>robbers</u>
Eight Words Describing Solution

Steps Used in the Strategy

1. Select a general category and list some words within the category. One example is the term *transportation.* Of that general category, car, bicycle, and airplane are all examples of modes of transportation.
2. List some features common to each word and one or more unique features of each word. For *transportation,* some of the features include two wheels, wings, uses fuel, has an engine, and carries passengers. You may suggest a feature or two and ask the students to think of other features. Provide examples, so that students will be better able to think of other features.
3. Ask the students to determine which features fit which words. Have them make an "x" or a "+" for features that fit and a "−" for features that do not describe the word. Use different colors for clarification.
4. Ask students to explain their rationale for each word. Then ask students how the terms are similar and how they are different.
5. Complete and explore the matrix. Have students describe the relationship and uniqueness of words. Keep the focus on comparing and contrasting features.

Additional Information

Another way to introduce Semantic Feature Analysis is to ask students to use their own names as terms to describe. For features, they might use such ideas as "has a brother," "owns a pet," or "has freckles." Students can have fun using a Semantic Feature Analysis and can get to know each other. Semantic Feature Analysis is an effective visual strategy. Teachers should model the use of this strategy until students are familiar with the process. Semantic Feature Analysis is used as a postreading strategy.

2.19   TOAST (TEST, ORGANIZE, ANCHOR, SAY, AND TEST)

Desired Outcome

This strategy (Dana & Rodriguez, 1992) is a study system that is designed to make learning vocabulary more effective.

General Overview

Test, Organize, Anchor, Say, and Test (TOAST) is a strategy that helps students learn vocabulary in a more effective manner. It is recommended for the early elementary grades through high school. This is a good method for getting students actively involved in the study of words.

FIGURE 1 in Strategy 2.18
Example: Semantic Feature Analysis Grid

Vegetables	Green	Have Peelings	Eaten Raw	Have Seeds
Potatoes	−	+	+	?
Carrots	−	+	+	−
Tomatoes	− +	+	− +	+
Broccoli	+	?	+	−
Squash	+ −	+	+	+
Cabbage	+	−	+	−

FIGURE 2 in Strategy 2.18

Feature Analysis for Playground Games

Kinds	Features				
	Games Involving Running	Games Involving Bases	Games Involving Balls	Games Involving Following Directions	Games Involving Touching
Tag	Yes	Maybe	Maybe	No	Yes
Red Rover	Yes	No	No	Yes	Yes
Hopscotch	No	No	No	Yes	No
Mother May I?	Maybe	No	No	Yes	No
Red Light, Green Light, 1, 2, 3!	Yes	No	No	Yes	Yes
Kickball	Yes	Yes	Yes	Yes	Yes
Spud	Yes	No	Yes	Yes	No

FIGURE 3 in Strategy 2.18
Semantic Feature Analysis

Students	Lori	Joan	Manda	Monica
Has brown hair	X	X		
Has blonde hair			X	X
Is a full-time grad student	X	X	X	X
Is in the education program	X		X	X
Is married		X		
Is tall	X	X		X
Has brown eyes	X	X		X
Has blue eyes			X	
Is VERY smart	X	X	X	X
Has a bachelor's degree	X	X	X	X

Steps Used in the Strategy

1. *T: Test.* Instruct students to self-test to determine which vocabulary terms they cannot spell, define, or use in sentences.
2. *O: Organize.* Encourage students to organize these words into semantically related groups; arrange words into categories by structure or function, such as those that sound alike or are the same part of speech. Categorize words as somewhat familiar or completely unfamiliar.
3. *A: Anchor.* Have students "anchor" the words in memory by using a keyword method (assigning a picture and caption to the vocabulary term), by tape recording definitions, or by mixing the words on cards and ordering them from difficult to easy.
4. *S: Say.* Pair students to review the words by spelling them, saying their definitions, and using them in sentences. Begin the first review session 5 to 10 minutes after initial study and follow at intervals by several more.
5. *T: Test.* Immediately after each review, have students self-administer a posttest, in which they spell, define, and use in context all the vocabulary terms with which they originally had difficulty. Allow the response to be oral, written, or silent thought.

Additional Information

This strategy is incredibly time-consuming. Most teachers would not have this much time to dedicate to vocabulary words. If the words were in a novel they were going to be reading, it would be more useful. It is an excellent strategy but not particularly efficient during precious classroom time.

2.20   VISUAL GUESSING GAME

Desired Outcome

This strategy develops background knowledge, generates curiosity, and increases communication among student, teacher, and fellow students.

General Overview

This strategy encourages and motivates students to learn more. Lessons are elaborated on to give meaning to new learning and reading.

Steps Used in the Strategy

1. Bring in visuals that the students can touch and hold to start the discussion for the upcoming lesson.

2. At this step, allow the students to ask questions. The more unique the visual(s), the better.
3. Stop conversation, so that there are still unanswered questions to explore in the upcoming activities.
4. With your students, decide on six activities that will help find the solution to unanswered questions. Have about three of your own, in case the students' suggestions are not appropriate.
5. After all the activities have been completed, bring the class back together as a group. Use this time to discuss what was learned and what might still remain unanswered.

Additional Information

Additional materials should be available. If time is of the essence, students can divide into groups. Each group can then be responsible for answering one question. Later, they can share their information with other groups.

Chapter
3

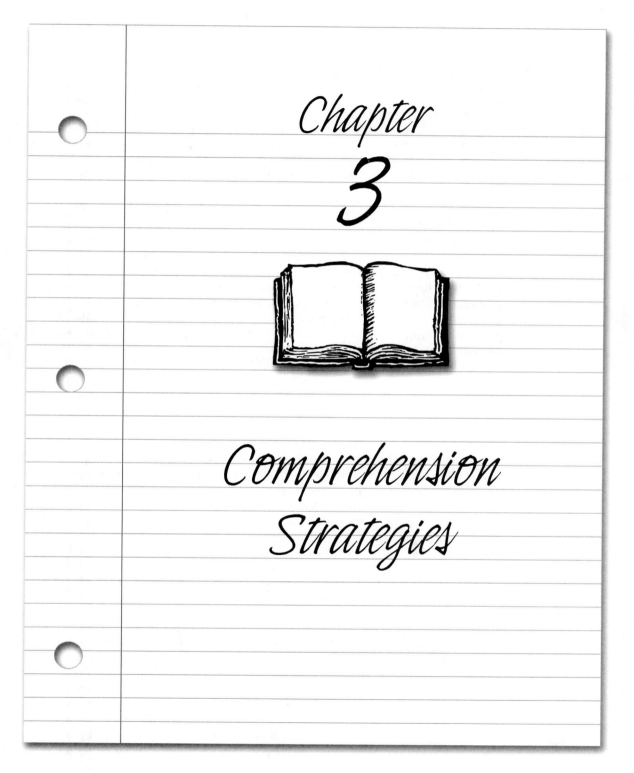

Comprehension Strategies

3.1   ANTICIPATION GUIDE

Desired Outcome

This strategy (Erickson, Hubler, Bean, Smith, & McKenzie, 1987) improves critical thinking and prepares students for reading by asking them to react to a series of statements related to the content of the material. In reacting to these statements, students anticipate what the content of the material will be.

General Overview

An Anticipation Guide consisting of a number of declarative statements can be used at the beginning of a chapter. The teacher gives the students a number of statements and asks them whether they agree or disagree with each one. This is done so that students realize that they *do* already possess knowledge that will help them to comprehend the material better. This guide enables them to connect what they already know with the new information. The Anticipation Guide enhances student comprehension by having them react to statements about a topic before they read the selection. It activates prior knowledge as a motivational device to get students involved in the upcoming material. The Anticipation Guide can be used with both expository and narrative writing, and it can be applied to any grade level. It can also be helpful when preparing for field trips, guest speakers, and film strips.

Steps Used in the Strategy

1. Read the material and identify its major concepts.
2. Anticipate the prior knowledge of students on the topic being presented.
3. Considering the significant concepts, compose up to 10 broad statements. The most effective statements are those which contain information of which the students have sufficient background knowledge to be able to understand their significance.
4. Present the statements to the students in the same chronological order as they will be found in the reading material.
5. Place the guide on a chalkboard, an overhead, or a handout so it will be available to the entire class. Read the directions aloud to the students.
6. As a class, discuss each statement briefly and ask students either to agree or to disagree with each statement given. Encourage students to evaluate their answers and listen to opinions from their peers. Make sure that students do not wander from the topic.
7. After discussing the statements, have the students read the text.
8. On completing the reading, have the students respond once again to the statements. Encourage student responses that are different from those earlier ones because now they are based on the actual text. If the students do not agree with the author, encourage them to substantiate their conclusions based on information in the text. Focus the postreading discussion on the

comparison of the statements in the Anticipation Guide before and after reading the material.

Additional Information

When appropriate, students should use other references as part of their discussion. This is especially true for gifted students or when the topic is not thoroughly discussed in the reading. This strategy is particularly effective for students who have trouble comprehending, because the guide encourages them to participate in lively discussion, which motivates reading.

The students should be aware that all the ideas they just discussed are going to appear in this reading. Then, after the students read the selection, the statements should be reevaluated. Discussion should focus on whether the new information has altered their reaction to the statements in the Anticipation Guide or the material supports their earlier reaction.

3.2   CAPTIONED VIDEO

Desired Outcome

The desired outcome of this strategy (Beentjes & Van Der Voort, 1988; Gambrell & Koskinen, 1993; Goldman & Goldman, 1988) is to enhance students' comprehension, vocabulary, and motivation in reading.

General Overview

This strategy (the video) can be used to supplement the basic reading instructional program, because it provides students with highly motivating reading activities. With this strategy, the audio and visual aspects lend meaning to the printed word and provide students the opportunity to view the video action, hear the spoken word, and see the printed text. It can be used at all grade levels.

Steps Used in the Strategy

1. Choose a video or television program with closed captioning.
2. Instruct students to read the captions as they watch and listen to the program. (The sound can be turned down for just closed captioned reading.)
3. Discuss the program after viewing.

Additional Information

There are numerous activity possibilities after viewing the program, including vocabulary activities and review of the video with the sound turned off. It is important

Directions: The book you will be reading is called *The Giving Tree.* Pretend that you were the author of this book and check the statements that are true to the story and important lessons for your readers to learn. After reading the book, review the statements. Which statements are true about the lessons taught in the story? Correct the incorrect statements.

**Before
You Read**

**After
You Read**

1. It is better to give than to receive.

2. A tree can be a friend.

3. It is important to have a friend.

4. Friends like to feel needed by us.

5. We feel good when we give to others.

Directions: You will be reading a story about Lightfoot the Deer. Pretend that you are an animal in the forest and check the statements that you think are important lessons to be taught in the story. After reading the story, go back and check the statements you found to be true in your reading. Correct the incorrect sentences.

**Before
You Read**   **After
                                                                         You Read**

1. You should take all the time you need to complete a project.

2. Shortcuts are better than taking the long way.

3. Where there's a will, there's a way.

4. People learn from their own mistakes.

5. There is power in numbers.

6. You get more done if you do it alone.

to know the equipment, select a high-interest video, preview the video, locate related texts, introduce the video, provide opportunities for reviewing, and create a video library.

3.3   CHARACTER ANALYSIS

Desired Outcome

The purpose of this strategy (Duncan, 1993) is to enhance students' understanding and appreciation of stories by examining specific characters within the work.

General Overview

Using graphic organizers, students compare characters as presented in the text and in a film.

Steps Used in the Strategy

1. Have students list characters' qualities to compare and contrast how they are presented in the text versus how they are presented on film.
2. Have students construct Venn diagrams to show differences and similarities. Model construction of these diagrams.
3. Have students share their diagrams with the class. Discuss similarities and differences.

Additional Information

This strategy helps students analyze the extent to which differences in the portrayal of characters may be affected by the selection of the media. The characters' actions, dialogue, and personalities form a basis for discussion.

3.4   CHORAL READING

Desired Outcome

The desired outcome of this strategy (McCauley & McCauley, 1992) is to allow all children to participate in a reading environment where there is no failure and no tension. This reading practice in a low-stress environment leads to increased word identification, fluency, and meaning; improved diction, and increased comprehension.

FIGURE 1 in Strategy 3.3

Character Analysis—Venn Diagram of Robin Hood: The Legend, the Disney Cartoon, and the Movie *Robin Hood: Prince of Thieves*

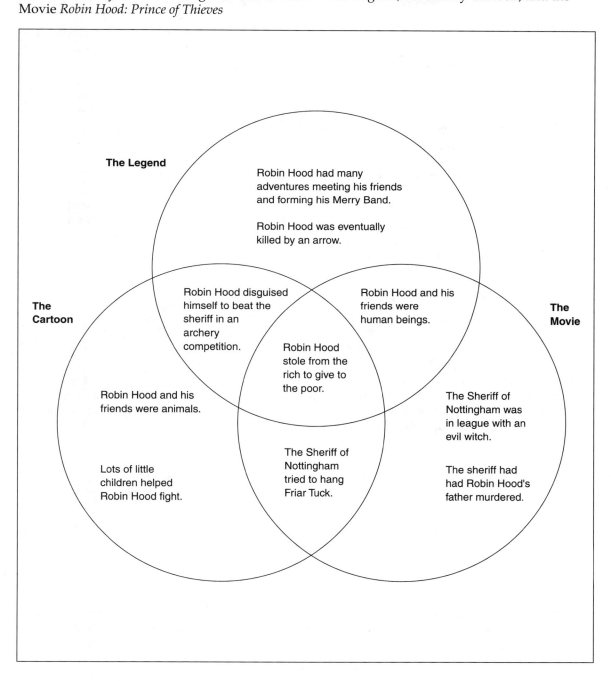

General Overview

Choral Reading is used to help teachers and children use language in a form that delights and excites. It makes use of voice combinations and contrasts to give meaning to a passage. All students read aloud simultaneously to promote comprehension, improve diction, and decrease the number of oral reading miscues. This strategy can be used with grades 1–12 for both English-speaking and ESL students. Any type of reading passage can be used, including poems.

Steps Used in the Strategy

1. Choose something from the content area or a passage or poem that is familiar to students.
2. Keep the environment relaxed. Your intent is not to produce a polished performance but, rather, an enjoyable experience with reading. You can invite the class to sit around a rocker or in front of an easel while they read.
3. Read aloud as a whole class. Make reading a positive, enjoyable, and highly successful experience.
4. Use discussions as a follow-up.

Additional Information

Alternatives are to add drama (expression, sound effects, movements, etc.) to the passage. This may help the students' comprehension. The strategy is appropriate for students who are rhythmically inclined, ESL students, or students showing reading skill deficits and who are too shy to read aloud alone.

　　This is especially enjoyable when reading a series in which the author repeats many words throughout the series. It makes reading pleasurable, and the students develop a positive attitude toward reading. Modifications can include having just the boys or girls read or a group of students read a part of a poem or story.

3.5   CREATING AN ANIMATED FILM STORY

Desired Outcome

This strategy (Duncan, 1993) enables students to engage in a fun and interesting activity that enhances their understanding and appreciation of stories.

General Overview

Film is one way a child learns how to give form to ideas and shape to thought. Students in the early primary grades can create their own animated film over the course of several days.

Steps Used in the Strategy

1. Schema development: after viewing an animated film, discuss the characters, setting, plot, and so on. Talk about movement of characters and animation.
2. Precomposing clay activity: allow students to work with clay in groups to develop characters for the movie. Encourage discussion of possible story ideas as students create.
3. Instruct students on drafting (making storyboard) with notes and sketches.
4. Allow and provide assistance to students in making the film.
5. Provide the equipment necessary for students to film the story.
6. Allow students to share their films with the class.

Additional Information

Stories and biographies adapted for film are easily accessed by students. Through the creation of films, story concepts are absorbed, making this medium important in the promotion of literacy.

3.6 DISCUSSION WEB

Desired Outcome

The purpose of this strategy (Alvermann, 1996) is to enrich and refine students' understanding of material that is read by getting them to consider both sides of an issue before drawing conclusions about the issue. This strategy also promotes critical thinking and increases comprehension.

General Overview

Discussion Webs are a graphic aid for teaching students to view both sides of an issue before drawing conclusions. It is a strategy that incorporates cooperative learning, it can be used across curriculum, and it stimulates thinking. It allows students to recognize that their beliefs and values may differ from those of their peers, thus promoting tolerance of others. The discussion should not be dominated by a few outspoken students.

Steps Used in the Strategy

1. Prepare students to read a selection.
2. After reading, introduce the Discussion Web with a question from the story (example: Did Willy deserve to win?) Partner students and have them list the pros and cons of their answers.
3. Pair sets of partners to compare reasons in reaching the group's conclusion.

4. Select (or allow students to select) spokespeople for each group and have each group report its conclusions to the class.
5. Have students write their responses to the Discussion Web question. Post the responses, so others can read and respond in writing.

Additional Information

This strategy works for all types of students, especially those who like debates. It is an effective strategy to use when there is an issue that has several views. Students should be encouraged to keep an open mind and should be reminded that it is permissible to disagree.

3.7   DRTA (DIRECTED READING-THINKING ACTIVITY)

Desired Outcome

DRTA (Directed Reading-Thinking Activity) (Stauffer, 1969) is a strategy in which students are guided through reading, making predictions, rereading, and confirming or readjusting predictions. This strategy aids in developing comprehension and critical thinking.

General Overview

DRTA is a pre- and postreading strategy. It engages the students in predicting what they think the story will be about. DRTA is a predicting, reading, and proving cycle. Because reading is a thinking activity, it involves having the reader use his or her own experiences to reconstruct the author's ideas. This can be used for any level of readers in group or individual settings, as well as with narrative and expository texts.

Steps Used in the Strategy

1. Give each student a copy of the selected reading. Direct the student to study the title and the pictures on the first page. Ask questions such as the following:
   a. What do you think a story with this title is about?
   b. What do you think might happen in this story?
   c. Which of these predictions do you agree with?
   This step builds anticipation and sharpens the thinking process.
2. When first introducing DRTA, familiarize the students with the strategy for dealing with unknown words.
   a. Read to the end of the sentence.
   b. Use picture clues, if available.
   c. Sound out the word.
   d. Ask for help.

FIGURE 1 in Strategy 3.6

Discussion Web: *Little Women*

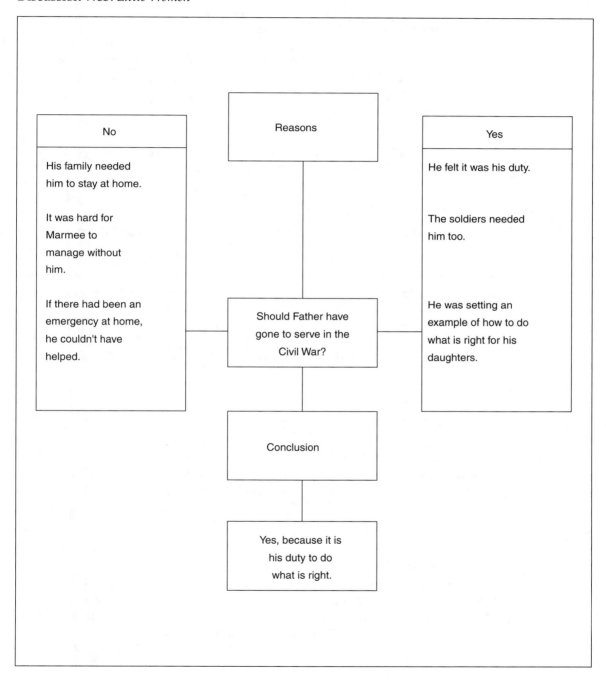

No

His family needed him to stay at home.

It was hard for Marmee to manage without him.

If there had been an emergency at home, he couldn't have helped.

Reasons

Yes

He felt it was his duty.

The soldiers needed him too.

He was setting an example of how to do what is right for his daughters.

Should Father have gone to serve in the Civil War?

Conclusion

Yes, because it is his duty to do what is right.

3. Direct the students to read a segment of the story silently to check their predictions. Ensure that students read for meaning. Observe their reading performance and assist students who need help with the words.
4. After students have read the first segment, have them close their books. Have the following questions guide the students' examinations of the evidence and the evaluation of their previous and their new predictions.
   a. Were you correct?
   b. What do you think now?
   c. What do you think will happen?
   Encourage students to screen their ideas and to make predictions about events to come.
5. Have the students continue reading the passage. With each new segment of reading material, continue the predicting-reading-proving cycle.

Additional Information

Unfamiliar vocabulary should be explained to students prior to their reading the selection. Also, students may find it helpful to read the passage aloud after they have read it silently. DRTA puts heavy emphasis on the reading-thinking relationship, which may be a novel idea to some students. It is important to model this strategy prior to having students work independently. DRTA requires students to be active participants in their reading. DRTA is useful for introducing new material. It can also be used with basal texts.

DRTA works for both good and poor readers to increase their knowledge-based processing. This strategy is appropriate from third or fourth grade through high school.

3.8   EPISODIC MAPPING

Desired Outcome

This strategy (Davis & McPherson, 1989) teaches knowledge of text structure, which helps students gain the ability to identify and follow major structures within the story, such as setting, plot, theme, and problem/goal/resolution. The development of these skills leads ultimately to increased comprehension.

General Overview

Episodic Mapping modifies traditional semantic mapping and is used with narrative text. It is based on the idea that most stories contain several major ideas, which follow a particular structure. Knowledge of text structure helps the reader remember the material, make predictions about what might occur next, and activate an appropriate schema. The five basic story grammar elements that students map in Episodic Mapping are setting, problem/goal, major episodes, theme, and resolution.

Steps Used in the Strategy

1. Explain that the main purpose of Episodic Mapping is to increase readers' understanding of a story by helping them understand how the story is organized. Encourage active participation through class discussion. Since each person's ideas about a story are valid, encourage everyone to contribute to the understanding of the story.
2. Teach each of the elements that make up Episodic Mapping:

   Setting: this defines background information—where and when the story takes place—and introduces the main character(s).

   Problem/goal: the problem or goal focuses on what the characters are trying to resolve or attain as a result of an initiating event that has set the story into motion.

   Major episodes: this is the plot of the story: the attempts that the characters make to resolve the problem or reach their goals.

   Theme: this section refers to the central idea of the story. It may be a lesson or an underlying thought that the main characters have learned as a result of their success or failure to attain the goal or resolve the problem. The "theme," as defined here, relates the events in the story to a broader set of concerns such as "Honesty is the best policy."

   Resolution: the purpose of this section is to organize the conclusion of the story in order to answer the questions, How has the story been resolved? How did the characters achieve or fail to achieve the goal or resolve the problem?

3. Model how you mapped a story that everyone has read. While mapping the story, try to explain why you mapped the story as you did. While your thinking may be different from some or even most of your students, through your modeling, they will get a "feel" for the kinds of thinking they should be doing.
4. Read and map a story together. Allow for a lot of discussion, as well as give and take. Get everyone involved and thinking.
5. Provide students with a story and a partially completed Episodic Map. Have the children complete it by themselves. After all of the students have completed it, develop with the students a "composite" map on the board, editing as necessary.
6. Allow the students to map selections on their own, incorporating Episodic Mapping into their normal repertoire of reading strategies.

Additional Information

Episodic Mapping can be used with grades 3–12 and with students with varying ability. Low achievers, as well as average students, have benefited from this strategy. It allows students to map interrelated ideas in a short story or novel, and it helps students visualize story episodes and comprehend main ideas.

FIGURE 1 in Strategy 3.8
Episodic Mapping

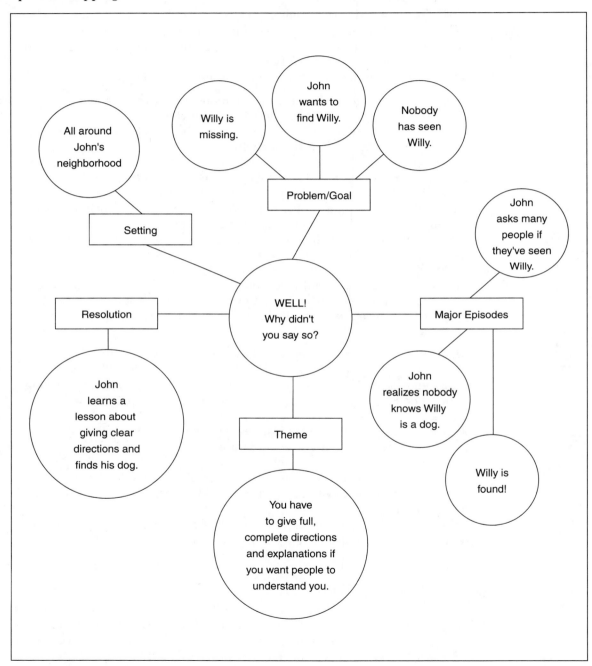

3.9   FIND THE FEATURES

Desired Outcome

Through the use of this fun, game-like activity (Castle, 1990; Richards, Gipe, & Necaise, 1994; Surbeck & Glover, 1992), students develop the ability to identify and understand key parts of stories. This ability leads to increased comprehension.

General Overview

Using story feature cards, teachers develop a game that provides opportunities for students to learn about key features of stories and their interconnections while emphasizing story content.

Steps Used in the Strategy

1. Begin by leading a discussion about basic story features. First, discuss basic story features such as the setting, characters, problem and solution, and cause and effect.
2. Divide students into groups of six to eight students. Give each group a color-coded card from one of four story feature card stacks: character, setting, problems, solutions. Have each group focus on one story feature, and write down on the color-coded cards as many examples of the story feature as possible. For example, the group may have five red cards, each one containing a separate characteristic name or several blue cards with a different setting on each.
3. Have several stacks of color-coded cards, each containing cards that represent a separate story feature.
4. Instruct students ("players") to take turns discarding and drawing cards. The students explain how the story feature cards are connected as they select new cards. The players must link the remaining cards. You may need to model this procedure the first few times you use this strategy.

Additional Information

Encourage students to collaborate and share thoughts with each other. Books can be used to verify connections. By using the color-coded cards, students are encouraged to focus on the relationship among various story elements and develop a better understanding of how these elements interconnect. The cards stimulate higher-level thinking skills and can be used as a basis for discussion.

FIGURE 1 in Strategy 3.9
Story Feature Cards: "Little Red Riding Hood"

Character cards are red. Problem cards are orange.

Little
Red
Riding
Hood

She and
Granny were
eaten by the
big bad wolf.

Setting cards are blue. Solution cards are purple.

In a
deep,
dark
forest.

The
woodcutter
kills the big
bad wolf.

3.10   GUIDED READING PROCEDURE

Desired Outcome

This strategy (Manzo, 1975; Spiegel, 1980) improves students' analytical and organizational skills, helping them become better able to gather and organize information from the material they read. Improvement in these skill areas also helps increase students' literal comprehension.

General Overview

This strategy improves students' recall of content information, ability to generate their own questions as they read, and ability to organize information. As a group, students read silently, then recall orally as many details from the reading as possible. They return to the text for additional information and organize the material in an outline form. Students discuss and relate new information to previous knowledge. This strategy can be used from kindergarten through college and with narrative and expository text.

Steps Used in the Strategy

1. Prepare students for the lesson by clarifying key concepts about the reading. Assess the students' background knowledge.
2. Assign a reading selection of appropriate length and ask students to remember all they can about the reading. Select narrative or informational material that is short enough so that most students can complete the reading comfortably in one sitting. To decide appropriate length for average readers, the following guidelines are recommended:

   For primary students, allow three minutes, or approximately 90 words.
   For intermediate students, allow three minutes or approximately 500 words.
   For junior high students, allow seven minutes or approximately 900 words.
   For senior high students, allow 10 minutes or approximately 2,000 words.
   For college students, allow 12 minutes or approximately 2,500 words.

3. After the students have completed the assignment, have them close their books and relate everything they know about the material they have just read.
4. List statements on the board.
5. Direct students to look for inconsistencies and misinformation, first through discussion and then through the material.
6. Add new information, and help students organize and categorize concepts in a loose outline form. You can also use webbing forms.
7. Have students reread the selection to determine whether the information they listed was accurate.
8. Quiz or test to reinforce the information.

Additional Information

This strategy works for students with poor organizational skills. It aids students in concentrating on their reading and encourages self-correction. It helps students determine relationships between concepts.

An additional step can be added to focus on metacognition. The teacher can pose the question, From today's activity, have you learned something about the best way to read? The point in adding this question is to get students to look at self-determination as a factor in personal reading-learning outcomes.

A modification to the Guided Reading Procedure (GRP) is the Guided Listening Procedure (GLP). Instead of reading the assignment, students can listen to the teacher reading. Except for the teacher reading the selection, the procedure is identical to the GRP. Teachers might decide to read the material orally if the students are able to analyze more difficult material than they can read independently.

3.11   GUIDE-O-RAMA

Desired Outcome

This strategy (Cunningham & Shablak, 1975; Flatley & Rutland, 1986; Wood & Mateja, 1983) improves students' comprehension, their ability to gather relevant information from a selection, and helps them develop a purpose for reading.

General Overview

The Guide-O-Rama presents a reading road map to aid in understanding content reading. It helps students process the major points and concepts of a passage while they are reading. They are instructed to highlight significant ideas, ask questions, think about an idea, and write a response. This strategy works particularly well for expository texts in grades 4 and up.

Steps Used in the Strategy

1. Determine an overall purpose for reading a particular assignment.
2. Select sections from the text that are essential to the purpose and that may cause confusion.
3. Develop questions or informative statements to help the students understand the section of text.
4. Present the guide to the students and explain its purpose as an adjunct to their text. Demonstrate the use of the guide by having the students work through a guide with you.
5. After the students complete the Guide-O-Rama, have them discuss their answers.
6. Display the class Guide-O-Rama in the classroom for future reference.

FIGURE 1 in Strategy 3.10
Guided Reading Procedure: The Civil War

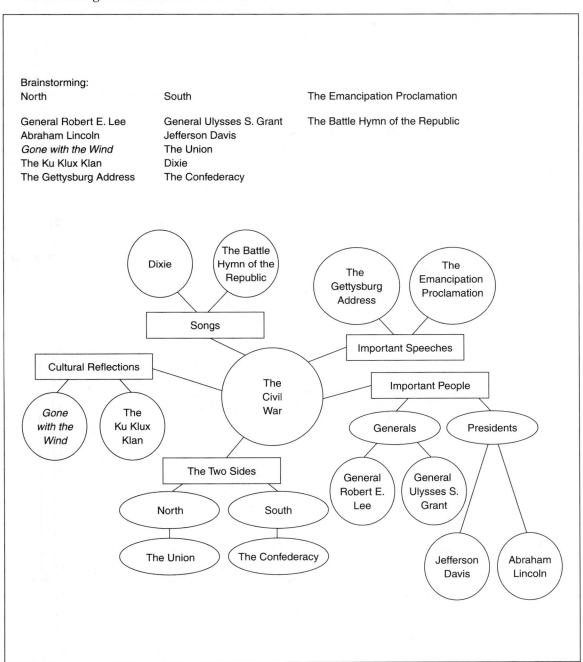

Brainstorming:

North	South	The Emancipation Proclamation
General Robert E. Lee	General Ulysses S. Grant	The Battle Hymn of the Republic
Abraham Lincoln	Jefferson Davis	
Gone with the Wind	The Union	
The Ku Klux Klan	Dixie	
The Gettysburg Address	The Confederacy	

Additional Information

It might help the students to work in pairs or small groups until they feel comfortable working alone. Small groups help promote discussion and learning.

3.12   INFORMAL BOOKS

Desired Outcome

This strategy (Robb, 1997c) helps students understand story structure by having them visualize and illustrate elements from familiar books.

General Overview

Students make informal books by creating and assembling drawings inspired by elements of favorite published books, such as setting, character, exciting or favorite parts, conflicts, and/or resolutions. Children do not *copy* published books, but they explore elements from those books that they find fascinating.

Steps Used in the Strategy

1. As a class, compose a list of elements that make a good story, such as funny/scary parts, what the main character is like, exciting parts, problems the main character faces, and solutions to the problems. Write each suggestion on chart paper.
2. Allow each student to choose a favorite published book.
3. Review story elements listed and have students apply a few of them to their story.
4. On a single sheet of paper, have students plan out their books by drawing a box to represent each page. Instruct students to sketch roughly, within each box, what each page will contain. Model this activity.
5. Approve each student's plan individually. Once this has been done, instruct students to assemble their books by stapling the correct number of pages together.
6. Allow students to illustrate each page of their blank book. They use their plans as guides. Encourage them to revise their plans if they have new ideas.
7. Encourage students to add simple captions to their illustrations. Captions will be dependent on grade level.
8. On completion of their books, allow students time to share and tell their stories to each other.

Additional Information

This strategy enables children to read and reread their own words. Art is incorporated into this strategy, which makes it fun. This strategy also teaches prediction and sequence in a story and forces students to think about the elements of a story while creating it.

3.13   INQUEST (INVESTIGATIVE QUESTIONING)

Desired Outcome

This strategy (Pearson, 1985; Shoop, 1986; Smith, 1985) teaches students to question the text they are reading. Development of questioning skills improves students' critical thinking skills, which in turn improves various skill levels, such as reading comprehension, listening comprehension, and the ability to comprehend print independently.

General Overview

InQuest is an acronym for Investigative Questioning. InQuest is a comprehension strategy that actively involves the reader or listener with narrative text through a combination of student questioning and spontaneous drama techniques. In InQuest, students engage in a series of oral language exchanges in the form of a news interview as they read or listen to a selection. One student assumes the role of a major character, while others become investigative reporters. As students ask questions, comprehension improves.

Steps Used in the Strategy

Preparation of Students to Become Investigative Reporters

1. View and discuss TV news reports (local or national newscasts) that demonstrate investigative reporting techniques. A single episode that shows both good and poor questioning is best.
2. Instruct students to evaluate these question-answer exchanges. Discuss good and poor questions, what questions are best, and why students need to be guided to evaluate the questions and responses. The following ideas about questioning are important to elicit during discussion:
   a. Questions that get longer responses are more desirable.
   b. Questions that receive yes/no answers can be followed by a "Why?" to generate a longer response.

    c. Interview questions generally elicit information, a reflection, an evaluation, or a prediction.

    d. A good interview should have a variety of question types.

3. Allow students to role-play an interview to practice these techniques.

Steps in Implementing InQuest

1. Read the story and establish general goals. Once you have chosen an appropriate story and have decided when the story might be interrupted for purposes of the interview, direct the students to read the story up to that point. Have students be mindful of questions they might wish to ask a particular character.
2. As a class, role-play the news conference. Choose a volunteer to play the character to be interviewed. Expect other class members to assume the role of investigative reporters, and the volunteer playing the character to use the information provided in the story to answer questions posed by the students acting as investigative reporters. In the early stages of using this strategy, you may want to model the role of the character/reporter.
3. Repeat Steps 1 and 2 at various points in the story.
4. Evaluate the interview. Involve students in evaluating the quality of the exchanges as a means of helping them plan future exchanges. For example, note good and poor questioning procedures for future consideration.

Additional Information

InQuest is a unique, student-centered comprehension strategy which builds comprehension. As events unfold, "what is known" is monitored by students who have learned effective questioning techniques. Comprehension is built through reader or listener interactions with characters lifted off the pages.

    InQuest can be implemented with basal reading material. It can be used effectively with many books read aloud to students. Narrative print, both fictional and biographical, is well suited.

    Interactions with characters, both real and fictional, transport the reader or listener across time and distance to view the action from the characters' perspectives. Characters become people engaged in real experiences. Investigating beyond the facts and between the lines becomes a tangible, active process.

3.14   JIGSAW METHOD

Desired Outcome

The purposes of this strategy (Fitzgerald, 1983; Heller, 1986; Pointdexter, 1995) are to promote comprehension of a large amount of material and to reduce anxiety of students that are intimidated by the length of material.

General Overview

This strategy promotes cooperative learning and enables students to comprehend large amounts of material. It is used as a postreading guide and is suited to the upper elementary and high school levels. It is especially useful for textbook material in content areas.

Steps Used in the Strategy

1. Place students into small teams (four to six members).
2. Divide the material to be read into as many parts as there are members of the team.
3. Assign each team member a part.
4. As members assigned the same material become "experts," have them work together to summarize the material.
5. Have the experts return to their teams and teach their section to the group.

Additional Information

Modifications can be made while "studying" by having students write sentences, lists, or research material assigned. The experts could report to others by making a study guide for their teams or orally presenting information. Also, the amount of text to be covered and divided can be varied to suit the students' level of comprehension. Teachers can also give a posttest following the comprehensive study to see if other students were attending and comprehending the material.

3.15 KWLA (WHAT I ALREADY *KNOW;* WHAT I *WANT* TO KNOW; WHAT I *LEARNED;* AND THE *AFFECT* OF THE STORY)

Desired Outcome

KWLA (Carr & Ogle, 1987; Mandeville, 1994) stands for What I Already *Know;* what I *Want* to Know; What I *Learned;* and the *Affect* of the Story. This strategy not only helps determine prior knowledge but also allows students to assign their own relevance, interest, and personal value to their learning experiences.

General Overview

KWLA focuses on elaboration and monitoring of comprehension. This strategy can be used during the prereading, reading, or postreading phase of instruction. KWLA can be used with either narrative or expository text. The sources of information are both the text and the reader, and instruction is implicit.

Steps Used in the Strategy

1. Make a four-column chart and label it as follows:

What I Already Know	What I Want to Know	What I Learned	Affect of the Story

2. Ask students to brainstorm what they already know about the topic. Write this information in the first column.
3. Ask the students what questions they would like answered on the topic. Write the questions in the second column.
4. After reading, instruct students to answer their questions from the second column. Write the answers to the questions and any other new information learned in the third column.
5. Use the fourth column to write answers to several sets of affective domain questions. One example of a question is: "What do I find interesting?" Have students reflect on the importance of information by answering such questions as "Why is this information important for me?" and "How does it help me to know this information?"
6. Explain to students that they may also use the fourth column to respond with new attitudes about their learning; for example, students may note that cicadas and other singing insects are held in great esteem by some Asian cultures.
7. It is important to include discussions. If you have students listen to the affective responses of their peers and talk about their own responses, then their written responses will be of better quality.

Additional Information

This strategy would be appropriate for students of all abilities from elementary through high school.

3.16   KWL-PLUS

Desired Outcome

In this strategy (Ogle, 1986; Weissman, 1996) students develop and implement schema (background knowledge) and learn the role it plays in comprehension. They also learn how to ask meaningful questions to help increase their own comprehension and develop the ability to read actively and to comprehend expository material.

General Overview

KWL is a three-step procedure used with expository text involving three basic cognitive steps. Before reading, they access what they *know* and determine what

FIGURE 1 in Strategy 3.15
KWLA: Plants and Flowers

What I **Know**	What I **Want** to Learn	What I **Learned**	**Affect** of the Story
There are many kinds of plants. Plants are alive. Some plants have flowers. Some plants have fruit. Plants need water to live. Many plants are green.	How do plants reproduce? How do plants eat? Why do some plants have flowers and fruit? How do plants help people?	Flowers and fruit are things that help plants reproduce. Plants make food by a process called photosynthesis. Bees help plants reproduce by moving pollen from flower to flower. Some plants create oxygen.	We should be careful about cutting down trees and killing plants because they make oxygen we need. Maybe bees aren't so bad, because they help make flowers. It's neat that plants are alive, even though they don't really move.

they *want* to learn. After reading, they recall what they did *learn* as a result of reading. KWL helps students activate prior knowledge and gives them a chance to reflect on and organize what they have learned from reading about a topic from one or several sources. They focus on what is important in the text to develop comprehension.

Steps Used in the Strategy

1. Step K—What I *Know*. Begin by having students brainstorm what they know about a topic you have selected. Instruct students to record what they know on their worksheet and add to it as they share their ideas. Record these ideas on a larger version of the worksheet on the chalkboard, chart, or overhead projector. Then, pose the following questions to broaden students' thinking during discussion: "Where did you learn that?" "How might you prove that?" When disagreement occurs, have students look for answers in the reading. If they have little knowledge about the topic, ask more specific questions.
2. Step W—What I *Want* to Learn. This is an outgrowth of Step K. As students share their ideas, note the areas of uncertainty or lack of knowledge that can be turned into questions. As discussion continues, have students think of other questions. Record all questions on the group chart. Just before the students are ready to read, ask them to write several questions on their worksheet that they want answered. Help students set their own purposes for reading. Questions can be added as they read the selection.
3. Step L—What I *Learned*. Require the students to write the answers to their questions either during or after reading. Help them either determine which questions they still need to answer or decide whether they have additional questions. Help students beyond the reading of a single selection.
4. To add the Plus component, have students categorize the information they expect to use.

Additional Information

The students have the opportunity to share what they already know about the subject, then decide what else they would like to know. KWL fosters growth in independent learning.

This strategy is used with small groups. While using the strategy, probing is essential to motivate the students. The information on the organizer can be used as a basis for mapping summaries.

KWL can be used with students at any grade level and with varying abilities. It affords many opportunities to assess students' knowledge at all steps. This strategy is good to use to introduce thematic units.

FIGURE 1 in Strategy 3.16
KWL-PLUS

KWL-PLUS Strategy Sheet: Animals

K—What We Need to **Know**	**W**—What We **Want** To Find Out	**L**—What We **Learned** and Still Need to Learn
– There are all different kinds of animals.	– How animals are categorized	– Animals are classified into two types—vertebrates and invertebrates.
– Some animals live on land, and some live in water.	– Why animals are categorized	– Mammals and reptiles are vertebrates.
– Some animals have fur and some have scales.	– The different categories animals are placed into	– Worms are invertebrates.

Categories of Information We Expect to Use

A. Vertebrates and Invertebrates

B. Mammals and Reptiles

C. Worms and Arthropods

3.17   LINGUISTIC ROULETTE

Desired Outcome
This strategy leads to increased student comprehension.

General Overview
This is a small-group discussion technique used with narrative text to improve comprehension through the use of discussion. Students periodically stop reading to discuss what they have learned. Linguistic Roulette provides a framework for student discussion and lets students have some control over managing the process.

Steps Used in the Strategy
1. Select a narrative text to use. Demonstrate the process of Linguistic Roulette, such as sentence selection and discussion before students use the strategy independently.
2. Group five or six students with varying ability into small groups for discussion.
3. Monitor the discussion initially; then let students manage the process.
4. Give students a time limit for reading a section of the narrative selection.
5. After reading a portion of a narrative text, have students skim through the section again, looking for a single sentence that they find interesting, important, puzzling, or special in another way.
6. Instruct students to write their sentences on paper.
7. Once all group members have read and selected their sentences, begin the discussion.
8. Have students read their sentences aloud and explain why they selected their sentences. This gives rise to interesting comprehension discussion. Invite group response.
9. After all group members have shared, have students read the next portion of the story and repeat the cycle.

Additional Information
Linguistic Roulette fosters comprehension in several ways. Stopping periodically to talk with peers supports comprehension. Students must think again about the story to select their sentences for discussion. Hearing others' sentences and participating in the small-group discussion encourages consideration of alternative perspectives.

3.18   PLAYING ABOUT A STORY

Desired Outcome

The desired outcome of this strategy (Galda, 1982) is to help students learn to enjoy reading while increasing their comprehension skills.

General Overview

In this strategy, a familiar story is enacted while the teacher initiates and encourages the students in their activities.

Steps Used in the Strategy

1. Read a familiar story to the class.
2. Prompt students to act out the story.
3. Encourage students to retell the story.

Additional Information

Students seem to remember, understand, solve, and analyze questions about the story after having acted it out. This strategy establishes personal contact with the story, resulting in greater comprehension.

3.19   PORTFOLIOS

Desired Outcome

A portfolio (Wolf & Siu-Runyan, 1996) is a selective collection of student work and records of progress. The teacher gathers materials that represent a student's work on a variety of subjects over a long period of time. The purpose is to document a student's progress.

General Overview

Portfolios are a selective collection of student work. They should promote student ownership, progress, and feedback, as well as information about student growth and accountability.

Steps Used in the Strategy

1. Assign an activity for the student to complete.

2. Select work representative of typical student performance and/or allow students to choose their best work to be placed in the portfolios.
3. Place the selection in a folder or another type of storage.
4. Give students feedback on the selected work or encourage each student or groups of students to supply feedback on the work.
5. Depending on the criteria established for the portfolios, give feedback on the selected work.
6. Use the selection as a representative tool for future work or as a review tool.

Procedure for Maintaining a Portfolio

1. There should be a specific purpose for gathering and collecting information.
2. The heart of a portfolio is student work, such as writing samples, reading journals, collaborative projects, and artistic creations.
3. There should be an assorted set of information gathered across a variety of learning contexts, content areas, and forms of communication. Otherwise, the full range of an individual's talents and interests may not be revealed.
4. Portfolios should represent students' growth over time and should inspire students to reflect on their work, thus learning from their mistakes.

Additional Information

Portfolios are meant to be modified. Each class or teacher may have a different use for the portfolios and their own way of choosing the material that will be put into them. This is a very flexible strategy which works for any type of student. Portfolios will benefit all students because they promote self-assessment and self-confidence as readers and writers.

3.20   PREDICTION BOOK REPORT

Desired Outcome

The purpose of this strategy (Robb, 1996) is to use good higher-level thinking. Students are taught to make predictions before reading the selection and then to assess these predictions after reading.

General Overview

This strategy is used to help students make predictions independently. As students read their chosen book, they pause and record their predictions in a notebook. This strategy is used during reading.

Steps Used in the Strategy

1. Have students write their names, the title of the selected book, and the author at the top of a blank piece of paper in a notebook.
2. Instruct students to study the cover and illustrations of the book before reading, as well as read the title and first page. Have the students record their predictions about the story, using complete sentences, and justify their predictions.
3. Either read the first two chapters aloud to students or allow students to read them silently. After these chapters have been read, have students record their predictions about the upcoming chapters. Require students to support their theories.
4. Encourage students to continue reading, stopping before the last chapter. Have them predict the outcome and offer reasons from the story as support for their predictions.
5. After completing the book, have students reread their predictions and make adjustments on a separate piece of paper to show how many predictions were correct.

Additional Information

This is an effective strategy for encouraging students to read and reread their own words. One modification is to have students use their predictions to write a new ending to the story, perhaps an ending that is totally different from the author's ending.

3.21   PYRAMIDING

Desired Outcome

The purpose of Pyramiding (Clewell & Haidemos, 1983) is to organize information in a bottom-to-top processing model that groups information according to details, middle-level ideas, and main issues.

General Overview

Pyramiding focuses on comprehension and organization. This strategy promotes interaction as students search for, discuss, arrange, categorize, and label ideas. Pyramiding can be used to review content during class discussions and to prepare students for outlining and taking notes for a written report.

Steps Used in the Strategy

1. Instruct students to read a chapter, section, or short article.
2. After students have finished reading, initiate a classroom discussion wherein students tell facts from the passage. Write each fact on large index cards, one fact to a card.
3. Display the cards in random order on a board for all students to see.
4. Have students sort the cards into groups and arrange the groups on one horizontal line on the board, which forms the base blocks of the pyramid.
5. Draw in the next step on the pyramid and ask the students to label the groups on the base line. The labels form the second tier of building blocks.
6. Draw the third tier but leave it blank and skip to the block at the very top of the pyramid. To help students name the subject of the pyramid, ask, "What is the whole thing about?" Write the subject in one or two words in the top block.
7. Have students agree on the complete sentence which includes all the information developed in the pyramid thus far. This statement is derived by asking the question, What is the author saying about the subject? Write this sentence in the third tier.

Additional Information

This strategy could be introduced as early as third or fourth grade and used throughout high school. This strategy could be used with all academic subjects.

3.22   QAR (QUESTION-ANSWER RELATIONSHIP)

Desired Outcome

The purpose of the QAR (Question-Answer Relationship) strategy (Chou-Hare & Pulliam, 1980; Raphael, 1982; Sandberg, 1981) is to teach students to focus on meaning in context. It also encourages students to elaborate on the information gained from the reading.

General Overview

QAR is used to enhance students' ability to answer comprehensive questions by giving them a systematic means for analyzing task demands of various question problems. It identifies the three types of questions asked: text explicit, text implicit, and scriptal. It teaches students ways to answer these types of questions. With this strategy, students learn that it is acceptable to reread to find answers. Students require a week of intensive training incorporating a minimum of four lessons to become competent in using the strategy.

FIGURE 1 in Strategy 3.21
Pyramid: *Tall Tina*

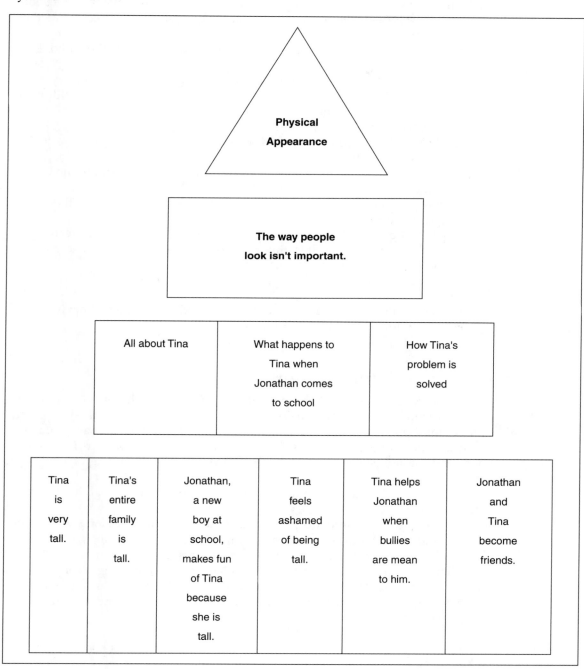

Steps Used in the Strategy

1. Introduce students to the task demands made by different types of questions:
   a. *Text explicit—"right there."* The answer to the question is directly stated in the material.
   b. *Text implicit—"think and search."* The answer is implied by the author but is not directly stated.
   c. *Scriptal—"on my own."* The answer is substantiated by previous information acquired by the reader or corroborated by reading additional information not found in the passage.
2. Give students three practice stages:
   a. Give students a passage to read with questions for which the answer and QARs are identified.
   b. Give students passages, questions, and responses to questions and have students generate a QAR for each.
   c. Have students read and determine a QAR for each and answer them (groupwork).
3. Provide students with review and further guided practice as they read slightly longer passages. It is important to give students feedback and have them justify their answers (group work).
4. Lengthen the passages. Make sure that students work individually on this step.
5. Instruct students to use additional material made available to them in the classroom to work on their QARs.

Additional Information

This strategy is targeted at grade levels 4–8 and is most helpful to those who have difficulty with comprehension. The teacher should model this strategy in a think-aloud process before allowing students to use it on their own. Visual aids would be helpful when teaching this strategy. Students beyond fifth grade may not need intense, systematic teaching of QARs. It may be enough to tell them about the labels.

The term "think and search" can be referred to as putting together the information in the text.

QARs also teach students knowledge of text structure. Students who do not understand how text information is organized will develop a sense of text structure and, from this, will learn how to locate answers.

This strategy is very helpful with students who are reading a content book (e.g., a history book) in which they are assigned to answer the questions at the end of each chapter. It is very useful to the student who does not understand what is being asked in the questions.

3.23   READ ALOUD

Desired Outcome

This strategy (Erickson, 1996) emphasizes comprehension, prediction, and the drawing of conclusions.

General Overview

This strategy is used by one person sharing a piece of reading material with another by reading the material to that person. It can be used with both expository and narrative text.

Steps Used in the Strategy

1. Read material to students.
2. Allow students to discuss and evaluate the material.
3. As a follow-up activity, have students create their own read alouds.

Additional Information

This strategy works best for students who learn better by listening and for those who have a difficult time with comprehension when they are reading independently. This strategy helps develop comprehension and can be used K–12.

3.24   READING PLACE

Desired Outcome

The goal of this strategy (Elliot, 1991) is to create a comfortable physical environment that encourages students' enjoyment of reading. Students evaluate their own learning strategies, which enhances their abilities.

General Overview

Reading programs such as this require much effort. In order to develop a Reading Place, equipment, furniture, and space must be available.

Steps Used in the Strategy

1. Pick an area that can be designated as the students' Reading Place.
2. Set up classroom space with a comfortable environment (soft chairs, sofas, lamps, coffee tables, etc.).
3. Add to the environment the types of items that help the students work better individually or as a group (tape players, computers, a printer, software, an assortment of music, and books).
4. Study the students' profiles to ascertain where they would most enjoy reading.
5. Continually look at the students' responses to the program to measure its success.

Additional Information

With this type of program, it is evident that financial limits are the biggest problem. In this program, students self-evaluate and become more aware of their learning needs. Having a comfortable, relaxing place to read makes reading more enjoyable for many students.

3.25   REPEATED READING

Desired Outcome

The purpose of this strategy (Dowhower, 1989) is to increase fluency and comprehension.

General Overview

Rereading, or practice and rehearsal reading, is a top-ranked study strategy which increases factual retention, leads to faster reprocessing of text, and helps students remember more meaningful structures.

Steps Used in the Strategy

1. Read the story to the group.
2. Help students construct a story map and summary of content.
3. Implement Choral Reading and echo-reading strategies to develop oral fluency.
4. Allow students to practice independently.

Additional Information

Rereading produces gains in speed and accuracy as well as better phrasing and expression, and it enhances recall and understanding for both good and poor readers.

3.26 REQUEST

Desired Outcome

This is a questioning strategy (Lombard, 1989; Manzo, 1968) that helps students develop questions and think critically. This strategy can be used with individual students or in large or small groups. When using this strategy, the teacher can begin by focusing on listening, speaking, and reading and eventually incorporate writing.

General Overview

The ReQuest procedure involves students' and teachers' silently reading sections of text and taking turns asking and answering each other's questions. This strategy involves all three phases of reading: prereading, during reading, and postreading. It helps set a purpose for the reading and monitors comprehension both during and after the reading. The purpose of ReQuest is to encourage students to formulate their own questions about the material they are reading and to develop appropriate questioning behavior. In doing so, students improve their reading comprehension skills, set purposes for reading, and develop an active, inquiring attitude toward reading. This strategy can be used with grades kindergarten through college and with narrative and expository text.

Steps Used in the Strategy

1. Select material on the students' instructional level which is also appropriate for making predictions. Identify points within the selection where the students will make predictions.

2. Build student interest in the procedure and explain how the procedure works by stating the following:

   The purpose of this lesson is to improve your understanding of what you read. We will each read the first sentence silently. Then we will take turns asking questions about the sentence and what it means. You will ask questions first; then I will ask questions. Try to ask the kinds of questions a teacher might ask. You may ask me as many questions as you wish. When you are asking me questions, I will close my book. When I ask you questions, you will close your book.

3. Participate with the students in the reciprocal questioning procedure. Read silently with them; then allow students to ask questions, which you will answer. Then, exchange roles and ask questions the students answer. During this time, demonstrate appropriate questioning and give feedback on the students' questions.

4. Once the students have read enough of the selection to make a prediction about the rest of the material, end the exchange of questions. Elicit predictions and validations by asking such questions as, What do you think will happen? and Why do you think so? If the students' predictions are

reasonable, move on to silent reading. If the students have difficulty making reasonable predictions, continue with the reciprocal questions. If after three paragraphs the students cannot comprehend the reading, discontinue the ReQuest procedure.

5. Instruct the students to complete the reading selection, reading it silently to check predictions. Provide assistance when necessary but do not interrupt the students' comprehension.

6. Select several activities that will engage students in verifying and applying the information they gained from reading. Follow with a discussion of students' predictions and encourage students to consider variations or adaptations of that story.

Additional Information

Although this strategy is recommended for use on a one-to-one basis, it can be modified to use in groups of up to eight students. For students who are experiencing the ReQuest procedure for the first time, a questioning game or activity may be useful as a starter. Students can underline ideas in the reading material about which they want to ask questions.

There is flexibility when determining the amount of material read before questioning and predicting. When using ReQuest in a small group, each student may be asked to develop a question. The role of the questioner may alternate after each question is answered. A variation is to incorporate an incomplete question into this strategy. The student or teacher initiates an incomplete question, such as "Why did Dave? . . ." The responder completes this question and redirects it to the initiator.

3.27   RMA (RETROSPECTIVE MISCUE ANALYSIS)

Desired Outcome

RMA (Retrospective Miscue Analysis) (Goodman, 1996) helps students become capable of talking and thinking about the reading process. RMA uses readers' miscues to reveal the strategies they use when reading and their knowledge about language. RMA is a small part of a reading program. It should take place no longer than 40 minutes at a time, several times a week. Through using RMA, students come to understand that reading is a meaning-making, constructive process in which they play a major role.

General Overview

RMA focuses on instruction during the reading and postreading phases. Fluency, word identification, and comprehension are skills that RMA emphasizes. Instruction is explicit. This strategy can be used with both narrative and expository text.

Steps Used in the Strategy

Child Reads Passage

1. Collect a traditional reading miscue inventory (RMI). Have the reader read a whole text orally without any help from others and then retell the story or article after the reading. Tape record the RMI. After collecting the RMI, do one of two things:
   a. If a reader lacks confidence or if you believe that the reader is not successful, then you may decide to preselect the miscues.
   b. During the RMA, you may involve the reader or readers in an examination of the whole reading if the readers are average or better.

Teacher Selection of Miscues

1. To preselect miscues, mark the miscues on a typescript of the material. Examine the quality of the miscues, looking for patterns that show the reader's abilities in using reading strategies and that show the reader's knowledge of the language cuing systems.
   a. Select miscues initially to demonstrate that the reader is making very good or thoughtful miscues. Initially, select high-quality substitution miscues that result in syntactically and semantically acceptable sentences and that make little change in the meaning of the text.
   b. Select word or phrase omission miscues in which the reader has retained the syntactic and semantic acceptability of the sentence.
   c. Select miscues that show good predictions followed by self-correction strategies.
2. Set up a series of RMA sessions with the student after selecting five to seven miscues for a 40-minute session.
3. Have the student read a new selection for a reading miscue inventory after each RMA session in order to show changes in reading strategies over time and to have new miscues for discussion purposes.
4. You should have two tape recorders. Use one to listen to the recording of the original reading and the second to record the RMA session in order to keep track of the student's changes in attitudes and beliefs.
5. During subsequent RMA sessions, select more complex miscue patterns that may show disruption to meaning construction.
6. With the student, examine each instance and discuss the cues she uses and what strategies eventually led to the expected response.
7. Help the student discover the reasons for the miscues and see how knowledge of language and reading strategies helps solve any problems she may have with the text.

Additional Information

This strategy could work for students of all ages if used incidentally throughout the school day to recognize the importance of discussing miscues. It works well to plan sessions during which students can discuss miscues and the reading process with students in upper elementary grades through high school. This strategy can even be used with adults who do not value themselves as readers.

3.28 SEMANTIC MAPPING

Desired Outcome

Semantic Mapping (Perrone, 1994; Richards, 1993) depicts the interrelationships of concepts in a lesson. It is a way to develop comprehension. Various kinds of displays can be printed on chart paper and kept. They are useful for introducing new vocabulary in ways that make it easier for students to remember them and in reviewing the words after the text is read. This strategy aids students' organization of text by visually helping students organize information.

General Overview

Semantic Mapping focuses on comprehension and can be used before or after a reading assignment. Mapping can be used as a way to encourage students to access their prior knowledge, as a way to teach vocabulary, and as a study aid. This is a prereading and postreading strategy that elicits a written response. The use of mapping works for all students but especially for those with poor organizational skills, those who have difficulty making connections between points, and those who focus too much on details and miss main points.

Steps Used in the Strategy

1. Use a small section of text, so the students will not get overwhelmed.
2. Identify the main idea of the content passage. Place it on a separate sheet of paper and circle it.
3. Identify the secondary categories. These can be subheadings or main points of the passage.
4. Connect the secondary categories to the main idea with a line.
5. Find all supporting details that relate to each secondary category.
6. Connect the supporting details with a line.
7. Connect all notes in a way that makes sense to the user. Model this procedure several times before students attempt it on their own.

Additional Information

It is possible to make many modifications for mapping. Students can make their own maps or create a class map. Unit maps can be made as an introductory lesson as well as specific maps for smaller topics.

This strategy will work well for all students. With prereading, they will brainstorm ideas to determine prior knowledge and, in the postreading, they will review the major concepts and details read.

This strategy can be modified in a number of ways, including the shape of the web (for example, shaped as a spider if reading *Charlotte's Web*). It can be filled out with words for vocabulary and should be made available so students can refer to it later.

Semantic Mapping is a strategy that can be used at any grade level, including college. It is a strategy that helps readers learn visually, and it promotes organization into categories.

EXAMPLE #1

Target word: *Tree* (from *The Giving Tree* by Shel Silverstein)

Parts	Colors	Varieties
wood	green	oak
bark	brown	elm
leaves	yellow	maple
roots	orange	spruce
limbs		cottonwood
twigs		evergreen
		ash
		willow

Actions	Products	Uses
blowing	houses	swings
bending	boats	climbing
breaking	fuel	tree house
swaying	paper	canoe
	wood	home for birds
	furniture	
	canoes	

EXAMPLE #2

Target word: *Sediments*

Location	Examples
river	sandstone
stream	limestone
ocean	conglomerate
on or under water	

Texture	Visual
gritty	see pieces of shells, etc.
rough	some look pasted together

FIGURE 1 in Strategy 3.28
Semantic Map: *Anne of Green Gables*

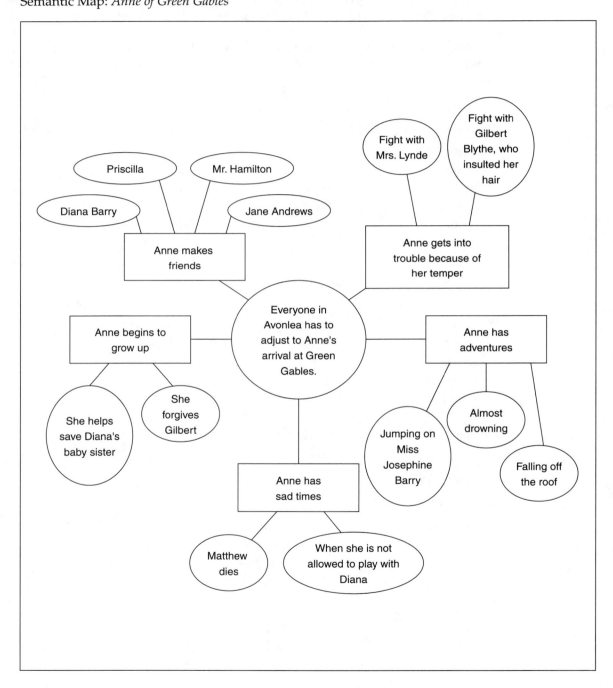

FIGURE 2 in Strategy 3.28
Semantic Map: "Goldilocks and the Three Bears"

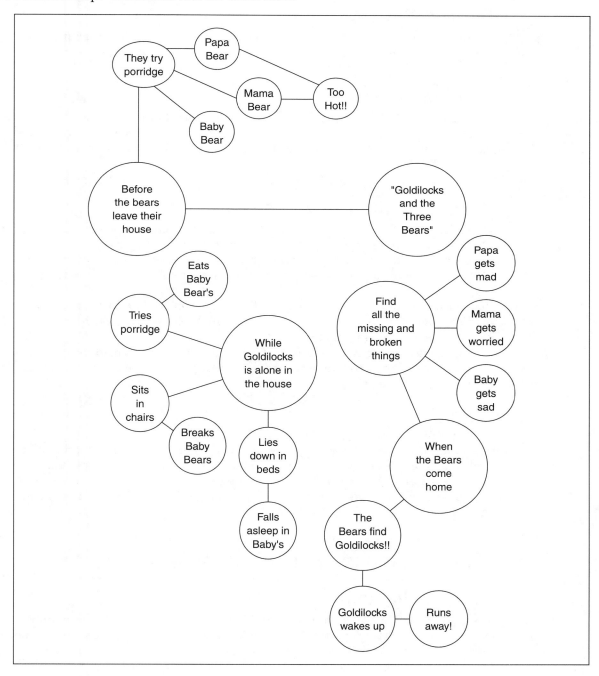

3.29   SHARED BOOK EXPERIENCE

Desired Outcome

The desired outcome of this strategy is to improve comprehension, listening skills, prediction, sight vocabulary, and grammar.

General Overview

The Shared Book Experience centers around the use of enlarged "big" books or quality overheads that include predictable stories and can be presented to a whole class or group. This strategy is used during reading and promotes the learning of print and language.

Steps Used in the Strategy

1. Pick an interesting book that you want the entire class to experience.
2. Have students sit in a very relaxing place (perhaps on a carpet).
3. Discuss the title and cover of the book and give a brief overview of the book.
4. Read the book aloud, showing all pictures and pointing to each word as you read.
5. Pause from time to time, asking prediction questions about the story.
6. Point out particular words or punctuation in the story as a lesson on vocabulary and grammar.
7. Make the book accessible to all students. Allow students to read the book to each other during free-time or reading time and encourage them to practice reading the book silently.

Additional Information

One modification is to have the students take the book home, one at a time. Students read the story to an adult or to a brother or sister. Taking the book home encourages reading at home and keeps parents and family members involved with the student's schoolwork. Parents then see where additional help may be needed and can try to help their child at home.

3.30   SSR (SUSTAINED SILENT READING)

Desired Outcome

SSR (Hilbert, 1992) stands for Sustained Silent Reading. This strategy is an important means of engaging children in reading. It involves a regularly scheduled time for children to read self-selected literature silently and without interruption.

General Overview

SSR promotes independent readers and provides opportunities to extend reading skills through practice.

Steps Used in the Strategy

1. *Establish a time frame.* Set aside a relaxing part of the day that will have no interruption—after lunch or recess. Start by having the class read up to 10 minutes each day and gradually lengthen the reading periods to a maximum of 25 minutes.
2. *Establish rules.* Everyone reads, stays quiet, and stays seated.
3. *Create an atmosphere of choice.* The children in the middle grades should select either fiction or nonfiction material that will take a week or more to finish. Younger children can have several picture books available in one reading period.
4. *Allow time to share.* After the class reads silently, allow seven minutes for students to share what they have enjoyed or learned from a book.

Additional Information

Readers of all ability levels benefit from and learn to recognize the intrinsic value of reading. It is important that the teacher read during this period. When the teacher serves as a model, students value reading more.

3.31   STORY CHARACTER MAP

Desired Outcome

This strategy (Norton, 1992; Richards & Gipe, 1993) helps students study characters in an organized way. By creating an in-depth character analysis, students learn how to recognize important information about story characters and increase their comprehension of both character types and motives.

General Overview

This strategy allows students to analyze story characters, actions, conversations, and thoughts. The purpose of this strategy is to help readers recognize information about the story characters and increase their reading comprehension through the completion of a Story Character Map. The strategy works particularly well for young and at-risk readers; however, it can also be used at any elementary grade level.

Steps Used in the Strategy

1. Display the "story character" map and an excerpt from the story, giving a detailed portrayal of the character.
2. Read the story excerpt aloud as students follow along with their own copy.
3. Point out that the author tells some important facts about story characters. Select one character. Highlight the important parts and model the author's thoughts on that character.
4. Ask probing questions to stimulate students' thinking.
5. Model the procedure for students.
6. Encourage the students to share their personal thoughts and opinions about the story character with other students or in a full-class discussion.
7. Repeat the modeling process, showing again how to analyze the character by his actions, conversations, and thoughts.

Additional Information

It might be beneficial to the students if the completed map were displayed in the classroom for future reference. After a few similar lessons, the students should be able to complete the map on their own or with a partner. Students can use these maps to help compare and contrast information about multiple characters within and between stories.

3.32   STORY IMPRESSIONS

Desired Outcome

Story Impressions (Afflerbach & Walker, 1990; Bligh, 1995; Clay, 1991) is a prewriting activity that develops a schema for ideas found in a story, and it provides a starting point for revision and for confirming ideas as the students read. Story Impressions can also be used after reading or listening to the story. The strategy helps students learn to retell oral and written stories.

General Overview

Story Impressions is a strategy designed to develop students' understanding of story schema and to help students set a purpose for reading by integrating prior knowledge and purpose setting. In Story Impressions, significant story clues derived from the important points of setting, character, and plot are chosen to guide students' thinking about a particular selection. Based on these clues, the students compose a hypothetical story summary before they begin to read the story.

FIGURE 1 in Strategy 3.31
Story Character Map: "Sleeping Beauty"

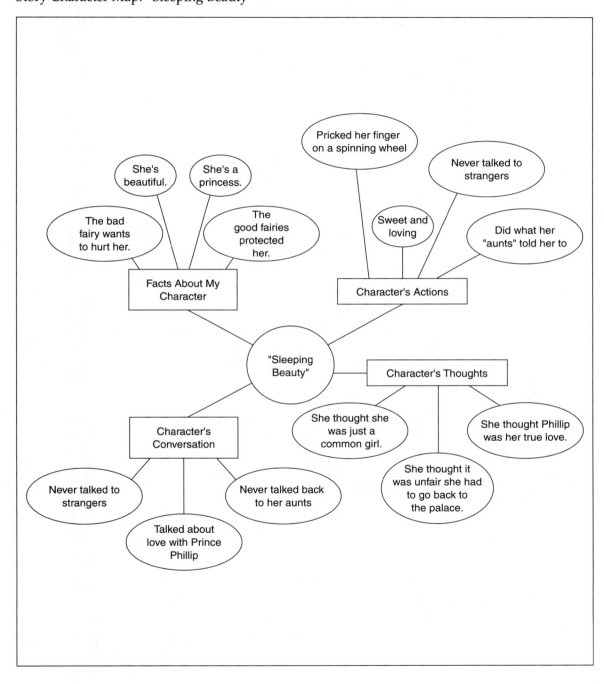

Steps Used in the Strategy

1. Develop a list of clues taken from the story. These clues should relate to the characters, setting, and main events of the story. The following is an example of a "clue list":

Laurie
Kindergarten
Parents
Stories
Charles
Hit, kick, yell

2. Read the title and clues from the story with the students and discuss any words that are unfamiliar. This helps introduce new vocabulary.
3. Instruct students to use the clues in the order listed to write a prediction story. Remind them that they can change the tense or form of the word to create a logical story.
4. Allow some students to share their prediction stories orally to a peer, to you, or to the class before reading the actual story.
5. Collect the prestories but do not grade them or compare them with the actual story or the retelling. Keep them as a writing sample or return them to the students for inclusion in writing notebooks.
6. After they complete their prediction stories, instruct students to read the story silently and write a retelling of the story using the story clues.
7. Analyze the retelling by using a story-specific checklist or retelling protocol to determine the important ideas and inferences retold.

Additional Information

Story Impressions can be started as early as first grade and used throughout high school. With first or second grade, read the story aloud and then have the students write, tape, or dictate their retelling. When the strategy is used in this manner, listening comprehension, rather than reading comprehension, is being measured. Story Impressions helps remedial readers improve their comprehension.

The focus of postreading instruction with Story Impressions should be to develop questions that stimulate critical and creative thinking about the story theme. Discussions should encourage students to share their views and ideas.

3.33   STORY FRAMES

Desired Outcome

Story Frames (Cudd & Roberts, 1987; Fowler, 1982; Gee & Olsen, 1991) is a strategy that uses cloze procedures. Words that are key points within the story are omitted.

FIGURE 1 in Strategy 3.32
Story Impressions: "The Three Little Pigs"

Three
↓
Pigs
↓
Houses
↓
Straw
↓
Twigs
↓
Wolf
↓
Huff, Puff
↓
SPLAT
↓
Bricks
↓
Huff, Puff
↓
Standing

The strategy increases students' ability to apply context to improve comprehension, identification, and retelling skills.

General Overview

Story Frames makes use of the cloze procedure by leaving out words or key phrases within a paragraph that summarizes a story. The strategy focuses on the story's structure to aid in comprehension. Story Frames gives students an independent guide for organizing and remembering information about the story. The strategy can be used with any grade level for both narrative and expository text.

Expository paragraph frames focus on content area material and help in reviewing and reinforcing specific content and in familiarizing students with the different ways in which authors organize material. This is a postreading strategy. Expository paragraph frames allow the readers to write about what they have just read, thus reinforcing the material.

Steps Used in the Strategy

Preparation Steps

1. Ask the following questions while reading the story: Is there an identifiable problem? If so, why is it a problem? Are there important events that contribute to the solution of the problem? If so, what is the sequence? How is the problem solved? What is the solution to the problem?
2. After reading the story and answering the questions, determine if the basic frame will work. If it does not fit the story, add or delete the appropriate parts.

Instruction Steps

1. Begin by drawing attention to the main elements in the story (characters, setting, theme, etc.) and print the features on a word card to help draw attention to these elements.
2. Have students complete a short story frame. Make sure to use stories that have an identifiable sequence in order to help the students understand sequence frames. Begin with half-page frames and work up to full-page frames.
3. Establish a purpose for Story Frames. Remind students that the purpose of Story Frames is to help them understand the story.
4. As the students become more familiar with using Story Frames, use more complex stories.

Additional Information

Students use their knowledge of story structure to organize story information, even when they are not completing Story Frames. As they familiarize themselves with Story Frames, their inquiry skills improve.

Students use story grammar language to discuss stories. As a result, they ask more significant and probing questions when discussing the stories. Students view the story as a whole made up of parts; thus, comprehension of the story is the primary goal.

This is an excellent strategy for students who have difficulties with comprehension. It can be used with all grade levels, depending on student needs. It also provides an excellent cooperative learning activity.

3.34   STORY RETELLING

Desired Outcome

Story Retelling enhances students' comprehension of background information before continuing reading additional material. It also promotes the reader's ability to sequence events in a story, auditory comprehension and listening skills, oral communication, and processing (Worthy & Bloodgood, 1993).

General Overview

Students gain comprehension by discussing material previously read. The students retell the story in their own words after reading it. It can be used at all elementary grade levels.

Steps Used in the Strategy

1. Read text story or text material out loud.
2. Ask students to retell the story, using their own words.
3. Lead students to state the sequence of events. You can prompt students' recall by using questions such as, What was the story about? and Can you tell me what you remember from the story?
4. After students volunteer their memories, resume reading the story where you had stopped.

Additional Information

This strategy is also used to "catch up" students who were absent or missed the previous parts. It can be used with expository text by having students retell a particular part or certain facts of a textbook chapter. Students can do the retelling orally or in written form. Younger students can also draw a picture.

FIGURE 1 in Strategy 3.33
Story Frames

Important Character

The most significant character in the story is _____

_____

_____

_____ . He/she is important because s/he _____

_____

_____ .

I admire the character because _____

_____

_____ .

Important Idea

The main incident in the story is _____

_____ .

It happened because _____

_____ .

Also, _____ .

Finally, _____ .

The solution happened when _____

_____

_____ .

Setting

This story takes place _____ .

The setting is significant to the plot because _____

_____ .

Words to describe the setting include _____

_____ .

FIGURE 2 in Strategy 3.33
Sample Paragraph Frames

Setting

The setting of this story is _____.
                                                        (time and place)

The _____ is an appropriate setting because
                    (time and place)

_____. This story could not have taken
                (reason)

place _____ because _____.
            (different time and place)   (reason)

Character

The most important character in the story is _____.
                                                                    (name of character)

_____'s most significant contribution to the development
                (name of character)

of the story was _____. _____
                                (reason)   (name of character)

was more important than _____ because
                                        (name of another character)

_____
                        (comparison of deeds)

_____ .

3.35 STORY WRITING MAP

Desired Outcome

This strategy (Bergenske, 1987; Stark, 1987) is a prewriting strategy which increases students' organizational skills and helps them identify and understand the elements of a story. This strategy encourages student creativity and helps students develop a purpose for writing.

General Overview

The Story Writing Map is a prewriting organizer that helps students transfer their story visualizations into organized writing. The map is divided into separate outlines that are pieced together to aid in the creation of a story. The Story Writing Map can be used with students grades 2–12 using both narrative and expository texts. It can help students locate the necessary parts of a story before writing or completing additional activities related to the book.

Steps Used in the Strategy

1. Have students work on the beginning, middle, and ending of the story in separate sessions.
2. *Part One—Story Beginning.* Instruct students to illustrate the story's setting, choose vocabulary to describe the illustration, and then write a few sentences outlining the more important elements of the setting. Explain to students that they are to repeat the process for the description of characters and the central story problem. When the outline is completed, have the student write the story's beginning.
3. *Part Two—Story Middle.* Use the same process to allow students to write the story middle. Review with the students the story beginning before developing an outline for the story middle. Have students illustrate the setting, choose descriptive vocabulary words to represent the setting, and develop sentences to outline the setting. As with the story beginning, repeat the process for the characters and central story problem.
4. *Part Three—Story Ending.* Repeat the same process with an outline sheet that designs the story ending. The story ending should contain the story solution and the conclusion.
5. When the students have completed their stories, allow them to share them with the rest of the class. Keep the stories available, displaying them around the classroom.

Additional Information

If the class contains some poor writers, it is important for them to outline and write the connected text for Part One's setting, characters, and story problem sections in three separate sessions.

Story Mapping can be used as a prewriting activity to help students organize their thoughts. This strategy can also be used as a postwriting activity for students to evaluate whether all the necessary story elements are used in their writing.

3.36   SUMMARIZATION

Desired Outcome

The desired outcome of this strategy (Dynak, 1996) is for students to draw conclusions and write a summary of text.

General Overview

This strategy improves students' skills in word analysis and fluency. It stresses the reader's ability to summarize the material from a text, noting important ideas, condensing text, and producing a shortened version orally or in written form.

Steps Used in the Strategy

1. Instruct students to follow these rules:
   a. Delete all unnecessary material.
   b. Delete redundancies.
   c. Substitute a superordinate term for a list of items.
   d. Use a superordinate term for a list of actions.
   e. Select topic sentences from those provided in the text.
   f. Construct topic sentences when not provided explicitly in the text.
   You may wish to model this procedure and/or present students with a handout outlining the process before expecting them to complete a summarization on their own.
2. Allow students to present their summaries, either to the entire class or within small groups or pairs.

Additional Information

This strategy can work for all students. Mapping could also be used to help complete the summary.

3.37   TELLS FACT OR FICTION

Desired Outcome

This is a strategy (Sorrell, 1990) which helps students improve their comprehension skills by teaching them to use a concrete, specific method before reading to develop questions crucial to understanding.

General Overview

TELLS Fact or Fiction is a guided comprehension probe used prior to reading. Students are taught to use the acronym to remind them of the steps in the reading process: T: study the *title;* E: *examine* the pages to find out what the story is about; L: *look* for the important words; L: *look* for hard words; S: identify the *setting;* and Fact or Fiction: decide if the story is a factual or fictional work.

Steps Used in the Strategy

1. Before reading the story, have the students read a step in the TELLS probe and answer questions about the step:
   a. T: "What is the title of the story?"
   b. E: "What clues about the story did you find after examining the pages?"
   c. L: "What important words did you find after looking through the pages?"
   d. L: "What hard words did you find?"
   e. S: "What is the setting of the story?"
   f. Fact or Fiction: "Is the story fact or fiction?"
   This procedure should take approximately 15 minutes.
2. Following the TELLS Fact or Fiction probe, have the students read the story.
3. Present comprehension questions after reading the story.

Additional Information

The TELLS Fact or Fiction probe can be completed by the entire class or on an individual basis. A chart can be used as a visual aid of the five-step TELLS Fact or Fiction procedure. Done as a prereading strategy, TELLS Fact or Fiction activates background knowledge.

3.38   THEMATIC EXPERIENCE

Desired Outcome

This strategy (Shanahan, Robinson, & Schneider, 1995) is a way of organizing instruction around themes or topics, instead of around subject areas such as math, reading, and history. By teaching thematically, it is possible to integrate instruction in meaningful ways across all subject areas.

General Overview

Thematic units are used to help teachers become more time-efficient in presenting content that can be integrated, therefore leading to higher achievement and better attitudes among the students. Thematic units are also used to reflect the real world, where learners combine the ways they learn rather than segment them into subject areas.

FIGURE 1 in Strategy 3.37
??TELLS Fact or Fiction??

Name: _____ Story: ___*"Jack and the Beanstalk"*___

Directions: Examine and read the story. Fill in the appropriate information in the chart. Decide whether the story is fact or fiction.

    T: What is the title of the story?
       "Jack and the Beanstalk"

    E: What clues about the story did you find after examining it?
       There is a boy and his mother and a cow. There is a really tall plant. There is a giant. The boy cuts down the vine.

    L: What important words did you find after looking?
       magic   beanstalk   giant   gold   harp

    L: What hard words did you find after looking?
       beanstalk   fee, fi, fo, fum   climb   beautiful

    S: What is the setting of the story?
       It is in Jack's house and the strange land where giants live. It is a long time ago and I know this because there are no giants anymore.

    Fact or Fiction:
       It is fiction. There are no giants, hens that lay gold eggs, or harps that talk.

Steps Used in the Strategy

1. Determine the unit objectives and goals.
2. Determine the theme or focus of the unit.
3. Gather books to be used in the unit.
4. Decide on student activities for the unit and the sequence of the activities.

Additional Information

This strategy works for students in kindergarten through high school. The Thematic Experience approach is appropriate for all students, because it helps them think deeply, pull together ideas, make connections among ideas, and blend subjects naturally.

3.39   THINK ALOUDS

Desired Outcome

Think Alouds (Baumann, Jones, & Seifert-Kesel, 1993; Herrmann, 1992) help students acquire the ability to monitor their reading comprehension and to use various strategies to deal with comprehension breakdowns. Think Alouds require readers to stop periodically and reflect on how they are processing a text. The strategy helps them understand and relate ideas.

General Overview

Think Alouds focus on students' monitoring their own comprehension. This strategy can be used during the prereading, reading, or postreading phase of instruction. Think Alouds can be used with either narrative or expository text, and instruction is both implicit and explicit. Information for Think Alouds comes from both the text and the reader.

Steps Used in the Strategy

1. Model five reading comprehension techniques:
    a. Form hypotheses about the text's meaning before beginning to read. Make predictions and show how to develop a hypothesis.
    b. Produce mental images by organizing information spontaneously. Describe to the students how you formed the visual images.
    c. Link prior knowledge with the new topic. Explain how you developed analogies and linked new knowledge to prior knowledge.
    d. Monitor comprehension. Model how to verbalize a confusing point or problem.

e. Identify active ways to "fix" comprehension problems. Demonstrate such "fix-up" strategies as rereading, reading ahead to clarify a confusing point, and figuring out meanings of words from context.
2. Verbalize each technique while students follow along. Demonstrate each one in detail.
3. Allow students to work with partners to practice.
4. Have students work independently.

Additional Information

This strategy works well for every student but particularly benefits students who have difficulty comprehending, because it helps them realize that text should be meaningful and that readers incorporate information from the text with prior knowledge to construct meaning. This strategy would work for elementary through high school students of all abilities. Think Alouds are appropriate for any students who need to monitor their comprehension.

3.40   VISUAL COMPREHENSION

Desired Outcome

The purpose of this strategy (Matter, 1989) is to enable students to use preexisting abilities to increase comprehension. It allows students to form mental images of the story, helping them recall the overall plot as well as specific details.

General Overview

This strategy is used to help students visualize and select the important parts of a story. Most students do not use visualization techniques automatically, but with training they transfer this ability easily.

Steps Used in the Strategy

1. Ask students to close their eyes and form mental pictures of what is being said or read.
2. Provide for the students a description of a place, an emotion, a thing, or a person.
3. Supply overall general concepts as well as supporting reasons and ideas, so that students have practice visualizing a variety of situations and story elements. Provide time for discussion and interchange of ideas.

Additional Information

If students are reluctant to answer verbally, they can draw pictures or write down responses. Students can create their own descriptions in cooperative groups to present to the class.

3.41   WEBBING

Desired Outcome

Webbing (Bromley, Schlimmer, & Winters, 1994; Sharp, 1991) is a graphic representation of categories of information and the relationships among them. Webbing helps students organize and integrate information when reconstructing story elements. Webbing encourages divergent thinking and discussion, and it is a useful prewriting strategy.

General Overview

This strategy is used to develop story elements, so it would be used only with narrative text, but Webbing could easily be modified to use with any text. Webbing emphasizes elaboration and comprehension monitoring.

Steps Used in the Strategy

Webbing to Teach Story Structure

1. Model Webbing as a prewriting strategy by creating a web of personal information.
2. Allow students to create webs with personal information and then write a letter of introduction.
3. Read a folktale and make a partial web, supplying problem, solution, plot, and theme.
4. Have students read the folktale and complete the web.
5. Instruct students to choose a folktale and make a partial web for you, a friend, or another student to complete.
6. To teach character traits, use a character web or comparison web to identify similarities and differences between two stories.

Additional Information

Webbing can be used with students of varying abilities in all grade levels.

FIGURE 1 in Strategy 3.41
Webbing: Personal Web to Teach Webbing Strategies

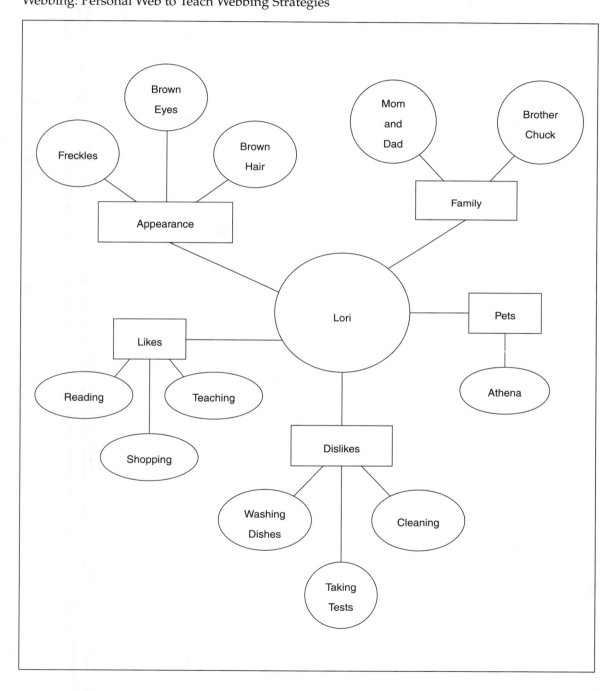

Chapter

4

Writing Strategies

4.1   3W2H

Desired Outcome

The purpose of this strategy (Manning & Manning, 1995) is to help students integrate reading and writing in order to interpret and explore the upcoming topic and material.

General Overview

This is an excellent strategy to use when beginning a new unit or chapter, because it enables students to look at a broad topic and develop a systematic plan for deciding what should be learned and how information can be obtained, as well as alternative methods for disseminating the information. The strategy encourages the students to be responsible for their own learning, because they develop the questions. Initially, this strategy should be implemented with the whole class, having the entire group form the questions. Gradually, students should work in small groups. Finally, students formulate questions independently.

Steps Used in the Strategy

Questions Students [Ask] Themselves

1. *W1: What is your question?* In this initial phase, have the students state what information they would like to learn from a specific topic. Depending on the depth of the material they will study, have them develop from 3 to 10 questions. Initially, ask for broad-based questions. Eventually, have the students take each general question and develop follow-up questions that focus on details in order to obtain more specific information under each general area.
2. *W2: What do you already know about the topic?* Next, have the students activate what they already know about the topic. For each question, have students brainstorm any information pertinent to the question. When done as a whole class, have students supply and activate each other's background knowledge. Write down pertinent information on the overhead or on the board in columns under the appropriate category, or develop a web to help students understand relationships.
3. *W3: Where can you find the explanation?* Have students ascertain how their questions can be answered. Have them first consider traditional sources such as textbooks, magazines, and trade books. Encourage students to explore other possible sources, including interviews with relatives or community members, e-mail, videos, films and filmstrips, and CD-ROMs.
4. *H1: How are you going to record your ideas?* First, model proper note taking, so students learn how to interpret the important information from a text. Show students how to record their findings that way. Encourage students to

explore other options such as sketching, graphing, videotaping, and audiotaping when recording information.

5. *H2: How are you going to share your findings?* When appropriate, give the students choices for presenting their findings. In addition to a written report, incorporate skits, posters, dioramas, debates, murals, and videos into the curriculum in order to add variety to the classroom. Allow students to select a method of presentation that is best suited to their strengths.

Additional Information

Although this strategy can be used at any grade level, it is more appropriate for the middle and upper levels, because it requires long-range planning. For children with reading difficulties, consider giving them the option of recording the information.

4.2   BUDDY JOURNALS

Desired Outcome

The purposes of this strategy (Bromley, 1989; Kreeft, 1984; Roderick & Berman, 1984) are to integrate reading and writing in a meaningful way, to enhance students' literary learning, and to promote natural communication in the form of written conversation.

General Overview

Buddy Journals integrate reading and writing naturally. When using this strategy, two students keep diaries and alternate having a conversation in writing. The teacher can provide a topic, or students can generate their own. Buddy Journals are interactive, as students take turns responding to each other in writing.

Steps Used in the Strategy

1. Provide students with a journal, the front of which they may personalize.
2. Have the students write in their journals for a week or two before having them share with their buddies. This will allow the students to become familiar with the expectations and use of their journals. Model how to write and date the journals.
3. For a period of time, reciprocate with the students in their journals, so they understand the process when they start alternating writing with each other.
4. When the students have had enough practice writing conventional journal entries, introduce the idea of reciprocating with a friend.
5. Decide how to pair students and change partners at least every two weeks.

6. Make students aware that the concept of journal writing is for the writer to share an important idea with the reader. Stress that spelling and punctuation are not the main concern.
7. Supply the topics or allow the students to develop their own.
8. Do not check the journals every day but monitor the process and make adjustments as necessary.

Additional Information

It is helpful to relate topics to what the students are studying or have learned. Buddy Journals can be used to express information or clarify concepts centering around a previously studied topic or theme. It is important to keep interaction meaningful for children to maintain their interest. Asking for volunteers, limiting the time for Buddy Journals to no more than two weeks, and using random matching to choose partners helps ensure positive student attitudes. Periodically, it might help students to return to solitary journal writing.

4.3   CURIOUS GEORGE

Desired Outcome

This is a motivational strategy (Richek & McTague, 1988; Stanovich, 1986) which encourages students to enjoy reading, to learn about story mechanics (plot and characters), and to increase their word identification skills.

General Overview

This strategy uses a motivational/predictable book series to improve remedial readers' (grades 1–3) word recognition. Students become familiar with characters, plot structure, and words common to the books. Assisted reading (Choral Reading) is used during small-group instruction, and then the students read independently at home. Additional literacy activities can be used to supplement the lesson.

Steps Used in the Strategy

1. Introduce the book you selected from the series and read it to the class. Then, read the story again by Choral Reading it with the students.
2. Orchestrate the reading by hesitating at appropriate spots from time to time and letting the students guess the following easier, predictable words, such as *curious.*
3. After reading, implement writing activities, such as making favorite word cards or the following:

    a. Letter writing to Curious George—you can write back as Curious George
    b. Predictable story book using sentence frames
    c. Drawing captioned pictures
    d. Writing their own version of Curious George stories
    e. Word cards to form sentences
4. After reading each published book together, develop a dictated book for the children to read independently.

Additional Information

This technique can be modified in several ways in relation to the activities that follow the reading. It can also be implemented using other series, such as "Clifford" and "Harry." It can be used in small groups, chorally, or independently. The following additional literacy activities can be used.

- Sentence framing: "Curious George is . . . "
- Writing of new Curious George stories
- Journal entries
- Drawing of illustrations
- Dramatic reenactment

"Curious George" Books in the Series by H.A. and Margaret Rey
Curious George
Curious George and the Dump Truck
Curious George Flies a Kite
Curious George Gets a Medal
Curious George Gets a Pizza
Curious George Goes to the Circus
Curious George Goes to the Aquarium
Curious George Goes to the Hospital
Curious George Goes Sledding
Curious George Learns the Alphabet
Curious George Rides a Bike
Curious George Takes a Job

Series Books for Beginning Readers
Allard, Harry. *Miss Nelson Books*
Asch, Frank. *Bear Books*
Bridwell, Norman. *Clifford Books*
Brown, Marc. *Arthur Books*
Hill, Eric. *Spot Books*
Hoban, Russell. *Frances Books*
Lobel, Arnold. *Frog and Toad Books*
Rylant, C. *Henry and Mudge Books*
Zion, Gene. *Harry Books*

4.4   DOUBLE-ENTRY READING JOURNALS

Desired Outcome

This strategy (Robb, 1997b) is used to build comprehension skills by drawing and describing elements from nonfiction reading material.

General Overview

Students make double-entries in their journals after reading a nonfiction book. On the left side of their journals they draw a picture that represents what they have just read about. On the right side, they write about what they have learned. This is a postreading activity.

Steps Used in the Strategy

1. Have students read books that relate to a topic being taught, such as simple machines.
2. Allow each student to choose an object or a concept from the book.
3. Instruct students to label the left side of their journals with the name of the object or concept that they will draw and to label the right side, where they will write, "Think Paragraph."
4. Have students draw their pictures. Encourage them to work from memory and to refer back to the reading for fine-tuning after they have finished.
5. On the right, instruct students to prepare a detailed explanation of how their object or concept works.
6. Have students show and read their entries to one another. Urge them to raise questions.

Additional Information

This strategy encourages children to read and reread their own words. Art is incorporated into this strategy, helping involve the visual learners. This strategy promotes critiquing by fellow classmates, which gives all students the chance to reveal their own ideas on each concept. Breaking down concepts one to each student, however, may hinder how much each student learns about the concepts she did not choose.

4.5   ELABORATION

Desired Outcome

The purpose of this strategy (Gammage, 1993) is to challenge students to elaborate on pertinent points while avoiding clutter in their writing. This strategy helps

FIGURE 1 in Strategy 4.4
Double-Entry Reading Journals: The Solar System

	Think Paragraph
	The solar system is outer space. The solar system is all of the planets and other things that are around our sun. The sun is a star. Stars are big balls of flaming gas. Someday our sun will burn out. But that's in a long time so we don't have to worry about it. There are nine planets in our solar system. Our planet is called Earth. It is the third planet from the sun. Some planets have no moons, and some planets have a lot. Jupiter has 16. There are a lot of things other than planets in our solar system.

improve story writing and vocabulary skills. Using elaboration while writing makes students' stories more interesting and reflective.

General Overview

The goal of this strategy is to demonstrate to students how strong verbs, nouns, and sound words can enhance their writing, so that readers can see, hear, and feel their stories.

Steps Used in the Strategy

1. Begin by writing a sentence on the board—for example, Mark Twain's quote "Don't say the old lady screamed. Bring her on and let her scream."
2. Using the quote as a guide for discussion, encourage students to talk about how they could focus their writing on showing their readers what *happens* in their stories.
3. Make a chart to illustrate the difference between showing and telling words, such as those in the following examples:

   Show
   a. "Aahhh!" screamed the teacher.
   b. Beads of sweat dripped down my face.
   c. "Hissss," whispered the snake as it slithered through the grass.

   Don't Show (Tell)
   a. The teacher screamed.
   b. I was very hot.
   c. The snake hissed as it moved through the grass.
4. Ask the students to select the sentences that helped them form better mental images. Encourage them to state why these sentences helped them.
5. With the whole class, make a list of "strong words" on a board in the classroom. Group the words into categories. Display a list of "strong verbs, nouns, and sound words"—for example, vivid verbs vs. boring verbs.
6. Encourage students to use their strong words while writing.
7. Allow students to share their writing with others.

Additional Information

Students learn how to *show* what they mean rather than just tell what happened in a story. By showing what they mean, students can become effective communicators of the written word.

4.6   GRAPHIC ORGANIZER—VENN DIAGRAM

Desired Outcome

The purpose of this strategy is to enable students to compare and contrast likenesses and differences.

General Overview

The Venn Diagram consists of two partially overlapping circles. This strategy is used to compare and contrast areas being studied. It has endless possibilities for adaptations and can be used in *all* content areas. The visual enables the teacher to check students' comprehension of material being studied and helps students conceptualize similarities and differences among the material itself, characters in the material, and so on.

Steps Used in the Strategy

1. Select two items or ideas/characters from the reading material that could be compared and contrasted.
2. Taking each item separately, brainstorm a list of characteristics/descriptions and write these under the item or idea. At this point, no comparison is made.
3. Identify a set of criteria to compare and contrast the items.
4. Once material to be compared and contrasted is determined, draw one circle for each concept to be compared or contrasted.
5. Each circle has an intercept point, leaving room where they intercept to write comparisons.
6. From the two lists previously brainstormed, lists of characteristics and descriptions of the two ideas which was completed in step two, have students select the words that include information common to those two ideas and place this information in the intersecting area of the two circles.
7. From those same two lists, have students determine information on how the items differ from each other. Then record this information in the appropriate outside circles.
8. The list of information for each character can be recreated for notes or future reference for study.

Additional Information

Many things can be done with this strategy. The basic diagram allows students to illustrate relationships between characters within a story or two or more stories, objects, math, science, and so on.

FIGURE 1 in Strategy 4.6

Venn Diagram: Differences and Similarities Between Aladdin of the 1001 Tales and Walt Disney's Aladdin

The Aladdin of the 1001 Tales:

Aladdin lives with his mother.
The villain is Aladdin's uncle.
Aladdin brings trays of jewels from the Secret Cave to the Sultan.

In both stories Aladdin gains three wishes from the genie. Aladdin becomes the Sultan.

Aladdin meets the princess before he finds the lamp. Aladdin has a monkey named Ali as a friend. Aladdin lives alone in Agrabah.

Walt Disney's Aladdin:

4.7 GROUP SUMMARIZING

Desired Outcome

The desired outcome of this strategy (Gee & Olsen, 1991) is to increase the reader's ability to understand and condense information. This strategy gives the student a purpose for reading and increases comprehension.

General Overview

Group summarizing is a pre- and postreading strategy. This strategy is excellent for the learner, because it integrates writing into the lesson. The teacher is a facilitator who encourages discussion by asking probing questions of the students after they give an answer.

Steps Used in the Strategy

1. Have students research the topic that has been selected for the reading. For example, prior to reading about armadillos, the class might decide to look for descriptions of armadillos, information about armadillos' food and homes, and other interesting facts about armadillos.
2. Have students divide the chalkboard into the sections they researched. Using the previous example, they would draw four boxes and label them Description, Food, Home, and Interesting Facts.
3. Once these sections have been labeled on the board, have the students look for these facts and develop a purpose for reading.
4. Direct students to read silently.
5. After the reading has been completed, ask the class to volunteer information for each of the categories on the chalkboard and record the information in sentence form.
6. As the information is recorded, encourage discussion by asking probing questions after each bit of information is given by the student.
7. Help the students develop class summaries from the information listed on the board.

Additional Information

Prior to implementing this strategy in the classroom, students must have already learned how to summarize information. The teacher must model this strategy in detail prior to assigning the class independent work. It is an excellent activity to use with cooperative grouping, and it increases research skills when used prior to reading.

FIGURE 1 in Strategy 4.7
Group Summarizing: Women in the Nineteenth Century

Categories to read for: what they wore, their roles in the home, their roles outside the home, their education			
Clothes	**Roles Inside the Home**	**Roles Outside the Home**	**Education**
Dresses It was illegal to wear pants. Petticoats Corsets Stockings and shoes Bustles All clothes were very confining. Bloomers	Raise the children Cook meals Clean the house Do laundry Supervise the servants (if they were wealthy) Make clothes Make other necessities (soap, candles, etc.)	Help with church functions Donate time to charities (if wealthy) Go shopping (if wealthy) Acceptable careers: governess, teacher, companion; if wealthy: none	Governess (if wealthy) Public school (usually not for wealthy girls) Finishing school or boarding school (if wealthy) Almost definitely not college Father, or brother's tutor

4.8 KINDERJOURNALS

Desired Outcome

Kinderjournals (Mulhall, 1992) are scribbles, pictures, letters, and words that have meaning on a piece of paper. This strategy helps students become familiar with the process of writing and builds their textual awareness.

General Overview

Kinderjournals enable the teacher to monitor students' comprehension. They can be used when students first start writing in the morning to express events that occurred the previous evening or immediately following a lesson by having students draw pictures and use words they just learned. Kinderjournals can also be used for assessment if the teacher develops a portfolio consisting of monthly samples that represent the progress of each child.

Steps Used in the Strategy

1. In order to develop the concept of page, initially use one sheet of paper daily. Drop the page limit when students have gained experience writing in their journals.
2. Gradually increase the time period students write in their journals. When introducing the journals, begin at five-minute intervals. As the students become more involved and sophisticated in their ability, allot increasingly more time.
3. Move students toward word and letter forms. Eventually, have print replace drawing and scribbling as students become more proficient with the writing system.

Additional Information

This strategy works for Readiness Kindergarten. Kinderjournals are effective for emergent and beginning readers. Children see themselves as writers immediately. When having students move toward the formation of words, write a sentence or word and have it available for students to use as a model, so they can copy it. Gradually, the students' writing more closely resembles the models provided to them.

FIGURE 1 in Strategy 4.8

Kinderjournals: Child's Writing and Teacher's Response

4.9   MIDDLE SCHOOL PICTURE BOOKS

Desired Outcome

When the students construct their own picture books, they learn to research and make important decisions while interacting with other students (Smith & Reed, 1982).

General Overview

Students are given the opportunity to create their picture books related to a science topic. They decide whether they will work independently or with a partner, what type of artwork they will use, and the topic for their book.

Steps Used in the Strategy

1. Think of a variety of possible topics you might illustrate. Either give students a detailed list of topics or allow them the freedom to choose their own topics.
2. Decide whether students should work alone, with a partner, or with a team of writers. Explain how decision making is an important part of the process. Make sure the students are aware that, if too many people are involved in the project, it may become more difficult to accomplish the tasks at hand and to create a first-rate product. Working in groups can be desirable; however, it is important to have the number of students in each group be appropriate for the project.
3. Direct students to research the subject matter. The students' work must not be solely artwork; accurate science matter must also be provided.
4. Instruct students on how to develop a storyboard. Have students develop a sequence of sketches to decide how their story will be laid out and what type of illustrations will be used.
5. Expose the students to many types of illustrations, so they are able to make decisions about the medium to be selected.
6. Help students develop a production plan. Require students to establish a timeline with checkpoints within which they must stay. Have students complete weekly journal entries to help record what they have accomplished and what they need to complete in their next session.

Additional Information

The students can present their book at an author's tea or another type of gathering where their books will be put on display. For younger children, a class book can be established. Each child in the class can construct his own page.

4.10   PROBABLE PASSAGES

Desired Outcome

The purpose of this strategy (Wood, 1984) is to increase the students' vocabulary, writing, and comprehension skills by integrating writing into the reading curriculum through the use of predictive strategies.

General Overview

Probable Passages is a strategy that merges the reading of a basal story with a writing lesson. The strategy uses key vocabulary from the selection. Students categorize the terms according to the elements of a story frame. Five major story elements are used in the complete story frame: setting, characters, problem, problem-solution, and ending. Students predict a story line and insert the categorized terms into the story frame to develop a "Probable Passage." After reading the story, they modify the predicted passage to correspond to what actually occurred in the selection.

Steps Used in the Strategy

Teacher Preparation

1. Select the most significant terms relating to the story and list them on the board or a transparency. Some of the terms may relate to the setting, characters, or central story problem.
2. Prepare an incomplete story frame. Categories may change with individual story content. You may want to provide a copy for each student as well as placing one on a transparency.
3. Prepare an incomplete Probable Passage frame. You may want to place this on a transparency as well as provide two copies for each student (one is used as a prereading activity and one is for postreading).

Strategy Steps

1. Present a list of key vocabulary words and read them to the students. If you think the words may not be in the students' listening vocabularies, then ask the students to repeat the words after you. Clarify words the students do not recognize.
2. Show students the incomplete story frame. Identify the parts of the frame. Ask students to slot the vocabulary words into the appropriate frames. Record student responses on the transparency as students record on their copy. Ask students to record further answers. Use some words for more than one category. Allow students to add words to complete the categories.
3. Show an incomplete Probable Passage frame. Ask students to provide vocabulary words from the completed story frame to complete a logical

Probable Passage. Ask students to restate their responses in concise terms to fit the space allotted in the passage. Encourage the group to reach a consensus. Complete the Probable Passage on the transparency while the students complete their own frame.

4. Ask students to read, or listen, to the selection to determine if their predictions about the story lines were accurate.

5. Ask students to complete a second Probable Passage after they finish reading or listening. Direct them to record the information as it actually happened in the story.

6. After reading, refer to the original story frame. Discuss which changes should be made based on information gleaned from the story. Make appropriate modifications while students change their copies.

7. Discuss postreading Probable Passages and complete one on the transparency as the group reaches a consensus about the story line.

8. Refer to the prereading Probable Passage. Ask students for comparisons with the postreading Probable Passage they completed. Which information was accurate? Were there differences? What were the differences?

Additional Information

Students of all abilities can complete a writing assignment using the Probable Passages strategy, because it provides a framework based on story grammar. This strategy uses key vocabulary from the basal selection to capitalize on students' prior knowledge of the topic and to stimulate their comprehension. Students can work in small groups to write their own Probable Passages and to revise them after reading. Working in small groups enables students to share their predicted passages and to see the range of possibilities that exist for a good story.

4.11   QUIP (QUESTIONS INTO PARAGRAPHS)

Desired Outcome

This strategy (Birkmire, 1985; Bridge, Belmore, Moskow, Cohen, & Matthews, 1984; McLaughlin, 1987) helps students learn techniques to analyze expository texts. Students improve their ability to develop and process expository passages and learn techniques to analyze key material.

General Overview

QUIP (Questions into Paragraphs) was developed to aid students in both writing and reading expository text. It involves three main steps that are organized and structured enough to make expository writing easier. This strategy can be used with intermediate grade students in both classroom and remedial situations.

FIGURE 1 in Strategy 4.10
Probable Passage Frame

Setting	Characters	Problem	Solution	Ending
A berry bush A turnip field	A hare A hedgehog The hedgehog's cousin	The hare brags a lot. The race	The hedgehog and his cousin trick the hare.	The hare is not so vain anymore.

Directions: With the information in the chart above, fill out the Probable Passage frame beneath, telling what may happen in this story.

Probable Passage
This story takes place mainly <u>beneath a berry bush and in a turnip field.</u>
<u>A hare</u> is a character that <u>lives by a turnip field.</u> A problem occurs when <u>he brags,</u> After that <u>he challenges the hedgehog and his cousin to a race.</u> The problem is solved when <u>the hedgehog and his cousin trick the hare.</u> The story ends when <u>the hare stops bragging.</u>

Revised Passage
The story takes place mainly <u>in a turnip field. A hare</u> is a character that <u>brags a lot about how fast he can run.</u> A problem occurs when <u>he challenges the hedgehog to a race.</u> After that <u>the hedgehog realizes he can't run nearly as fast as the hare.</u> The problem is solved when <u>the hedgehog and his cousin pretend to be each other and trick the hare into thinking that the hedgehog is running faster than he is.</u> The story ends when <u>the hare gets too tired to run anymore and goes home, no longer bragging about how fast he can run.</u>

Steps Used in the Strategy

1. *Interview grid.* Instruct students to begin by determining their overall topic. Instruct them to develop three open-ended questions relevant to the topic. Place the questions in the left-hand column of the grid and have the students seek answers to their questions. At first, use interviews with family, friends, and classmates as sources of information. As students become more familiar with this format, instruct them to use more traditional sources, such as reference books. Place responses in the appropriate boxes of the interview grid.
2. *Outline.* Use the complete grid to provide a smooth transition to the creation of outlines. Place the overall topic as the heading of the outline. Use inquiry questions for the subheadings and the responses for supporting details. Model this format for students.
3. *Paragraphs.* Model for students the process of creating an overall topic sentence by reviewing their questions and responses. Each heading becomes the main idea statement of a paragraph, followed by the supporting information. After the three paragraphs are developed, add a concluding sentence to restate the main idea.

Additional Information

This strategy is well suited to the compare/contrast expository format. Preparation of the interview grid and outline leads students to the awareness of similarities and differences. The paragraphs show the importance of such relationships.

4.12   REVIEWING A FILM

Desired Outcome

This strategy (Duncan, 1993) leads to the enhancement of students' understanding and appreciation of stories and film.

General Overview

Students develop their persuasive abilities by critical viewing, evaluating, and making historical comparisons of films.

Steps Used in the Strategy

1. Have students read several film reviews to familiarize themselves with the genre. Also, discuss the history of film.
2. After a guided discussion of film and reviews, give students the following instructions:
   a. Recall the film and consider your thoughts and feelings about it.

FIGURE 1 in Strategy 4.11

QUIP Interview Grid for "Clothes in the 1960s"

Questions	Interview/Reading Responses
What kind of clothes did teenagers wear?	**Mom:** Blue jeans with lots of patches (even if they had no holes), love beads, peace sign jewelry **Dad:** Tie-dyed t-shirts, jackets with fringes (twist jackets) **Mike:** Bell bottoms **American encyclopedia:** Mini-skirts, tunic shirts, "psychedelic" patterns
What could kids wear to school?	**Mom:** Girls couldn't wear pants or mini-skirts. **Dad:** Long pants (no shorts) and a shirt with a collar **Grandma:** More than they do today!! **Mike:** Uniforms. **American encyclopedia:** Most schools had dress codes specifying no shorts or hats. Girls whose skirts were thought to be too short had to kneel on the floor—if their skirts didn't touch the ground, they had to go home and change them.
How did grown-ups feel about kids' clothes?	**Mom:** They didn't like it very much—I used to get in trouble because my skirts were too short. **Dad:** Grandma told me that I was "no more than respectable!" and, even if my friends went to school looking like savages, I was going to be dressed properly. **Grandma:** I couldn't wait for your father and aunts and uncles to start dressing properly. **Mike:** They made dressing like a hippie illegal. **American encyclopedia:** Many adults did not approve of the new teenage subculture. Mini-skirts were not permitted in many schools and public places, such as restaurants.

b. Use the critic's jot sheet and note ideas under each category.
c. When the jot sheet is completed, cut out sections to rearrange segments for better organization.
d. Begin the first draft of the review. Consider the people who will read the review, and try to write persuasively.

4.13 SENTENCE COLLECTING

Desired Outcome

The purpose of this strategy (Speaker, 1991) is to improve students' ability to understand and write complicated sentences and to help them develop higher-level thinking.

General Overview

Students are active participants in this strategy and build confidence by displaying their sentence collection in the classroom for their peers to see. Students discuss their sentences with their classmates. This strategy promotes a reading and writing relationship.

Steps Used in the Strategy

1. Introduce to the students creative sentences found in books you or the students have read. These sentences could represent humor or sorrow, define vocabulary, set the tone of the story, compare characters, explain plots, and so on.
2. Write approximately three of these sentences on large brown paper and discuss them. Encourage the students to add their own sentences to the collection. (Use selected sentences to illustrate a particular type of sentence structure.)
3. Display these sentences around the classroom. Allow time each day for students to discuss the sentences and add to the collection.

Additional Information

The collected sentences could be made into a class book when taken down from the displays. A student could get extra credit for creativity or participation.

FIGURE 1 in Strategy 4.12

Reviewing a Film: Critic's Jot Sheet for the Movie *The Little Mermaid*

Jot Sheet   Movie: <u>The Little Mermaid</u>

What is your general impression of the movie? *I liked this movie—I thought that it was a nice fairy tale/love story.*

Why might a filmmaker have wanted to make this film? *To entertain kids and make people who watch it feel happy.*

What was happening in America when this was made? Did it influence the film? *There was a presidential election that year, but I don't think that influenced this movie much. This movie is based on a real story.*

What were the outstanding parts of the film? *The "Under the Sea" song, the battle with Ursula, and the ending.*

What were the weak parts of the film? *Where her father destroyed her secret place, Ursula pretending to be a real person to marry the prince.*

What was the quality of the film?
   Musical score: *Excellent! Lots of wonderful songs.*
   Animation: *Wonderful! It's very detailed and lifelike, especially during songs.*
   Big screen vs. video: *Everything is better on the big screen, but this movie is still very enjoyable on video. It would be cool to hear the songs with surround sound.*

How does this compare with other animated films? *This is the oldest of the "new era" of Disney films. In the past 10 years since it was released, animation has gotten even more sophisticated. The quality of the story and songs is still really good.*

How will this film be received by today's viewers? *Today's viewers will like it a lot, especially kids who want to do things that their parents don't want them to do. These kids will like this movie a lot.*

4.14 STORYBOARD TECHNIQUE

Desired Outcome

The Storyboard Technique (Harrington, 1994) is a prewriting activity emphasizing elaboration, prediction, brainstorming, and sequencing. It is used to motivate students to express themselves by first using art and then adding words.

General Overview

This strategy involves reading, writing, and illustrating. It is effective because it motivates beginning writers and readers.

Steps Used in the Strategy

1. Instruct students to divide plain pieces of white construction paper into many (six to eight) sections.
2. Help students brainstorm story ideas and draw beginning and ending pictures in the first and last sections of their papers.
3. Have students fill in remaining sections in sequence as they develop their story ideas. Model this procedure.
4. Check for sequence. Have students make corrections on their first drafts.
5. Instruct students to add words to their pictures and create final drafts.
6. You can have these stories laminated (published).
7. Allow students to share their stories with others.

Additional Information

A modification to this strategy is for students to cut out each section of their stories and glue each section onto a new piece of paper. They would then design covers for their books and assemble their books accordingly. This is a book they can be proud of and read to everyone. The Storyboard Technique works well for beginning writers, and it has been very successful with remedial students who experience difficulty in writing.

4.15 WORDLESS PICTURE BOOKS

Desired Outcome

This strategy (Swan, 1992) offers a valuable opportunity to develop literacy competencies in young children. Students are paired in a buddy system to develop writing, reading, listening, and speaking skills.

FIGURE 1 in Strategy 4.14

Storyboard Technique: Meeting Alexander Bear

Mary and John were walking in the woods one day after school.

Suddenly, they saw a bear! They were very scared.

"Don't be scared," said the bear. "My name is Alexander. I will not hurt you."

"Come into my house," said Alexander. John and Mary were a little nervous. His house was a cave!

His house was really nice! There was a lot of honey.

John, Mary, and Alexander play games in the cave.

General Overview

Wordless Picture Books is a strategy used to develop students' sentence comprehension. The strategy can be used at a writing center so children have better access to the books. The books also can be used in conjunction with the Language Experience Approach.

Steps Used in the Strategy

1. Model for the class how to read a book—turning pages, reading sentences, and so on and encourage the students both to observe and to be involved in the reading process.
2. Encourage the students to tell the story themselves.
3. Have the students buddy up and write their interpretations of other Wordless Picture Books.
4. Once their stories have been written, help students with editing. When the editing is complete, have buddies read their stories to their classmates.

Additional Information

This strategy is effective for primary grade, bilingual, and English-as-a-second language students, as well as for adolescent nonreaders. It is an excellent activity for the student who prefers to communicate through writing rather than discussion. Also, it helps students develop a sense of story line.

4.16   ZIGZAG

Desired Outcome

ZigZag is a strategy that enables students to brainstorm both the major elements and supporting details in a story. When incorporated into a writing activity, it allows students to produce a more cohesive, well-organized product.

General Overview

ZigZag can be used to interrelate reading and writing. After students read a passage, incorporate ZigZag to help them organize the material and create an idea base for writing.

Steps Used in the Strategy

1. After students have read a passage, present them with a paper containing the ZigZag format (see the example in Figure 1).

2. If appropriate, divide students into small groups or organize pupil partners. Next, have students write words from the story that represent its major concepts on each line segment. Gear the selection of the words to the focus of the writing assignments. For example, if the writing assignment is to emphasize characterization, have students write the names of interesting characters on the ZigZag. If the writing assignment is less structured, ask students to write words from the story whose initial letter matches the final letter of the previous word.

3. After the students have completed words representing the main concepts on the lines, have them write supporting details for each major concept in the space next to the ZigZag. Depending on the students' ability level and the difficulty of the material, students might list between two and eight details for each major concept on the ZigZag.

4. Have students use the completed ZigZag as a basis for a writing activity. First, have them select the major concepts they want to include in their writing assignment and eliminate the remaining ones.

5. Next, from the major concepts written on the line segments to be included in their writing, have students determine a sequence for their development. Students may number the line segments to represent the sequence. This will enable students to organize their writing and determine a logical order. Each word would be developed into a topic sentence for each paragraph.

6. After selecting and sequencing the major concepts, have students focus on the supporting details they have written in the accompanying spaces and determine which to include, as well as a logical order. The supporting details should be used to develop the paragraph and support each topic sentence.

Additional Information

ZigZag can be used with students of varying ability at all grade levels to help them organize the writing process and connect details to important concepts.

FIGURE 1 in Strategy 4.16
ZigZag: Example Lesson from *The Coconut Game* by Robert Riddele

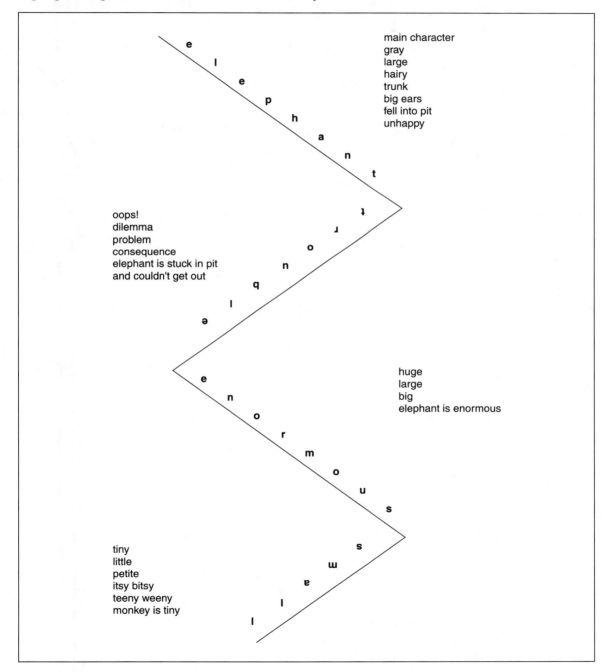

main character
gray
large
hairy
trunk
big ears
fell into pit
unhappy

oops!
dilemma
problem
consequence
elephant is stuck in pit
and couldn't get out

huge
large
big
elephant is enormous

tiny
little
petite
itsy bitsy
teeny weeny
monkey is tiny

Chapter
5

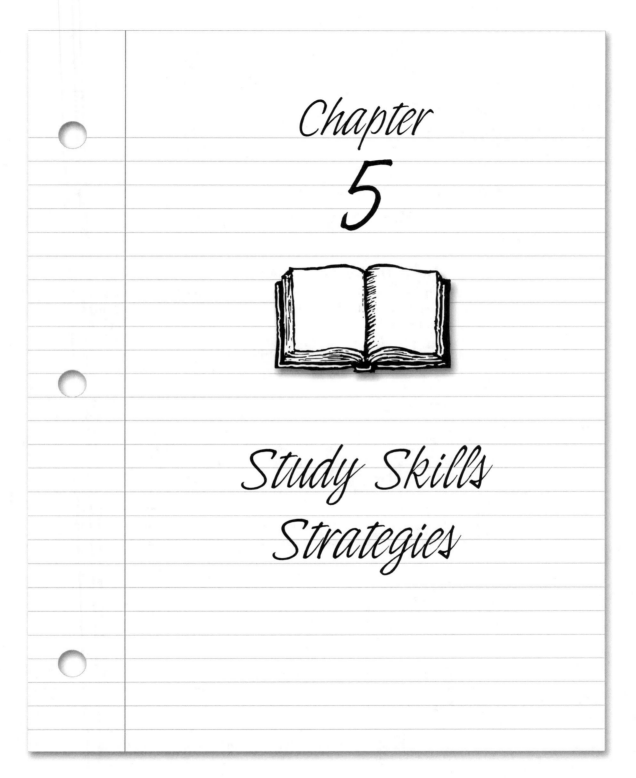

Study Skills
Strategies

5.1   FIVE-DAY TEST PREPARATION PLAN

Desired Outcome

The Five-Day Test Preparation Plan (Mangrum & Strichart, 1993) helps students prepare themselves better for tests and, consequently, receive higher grades.

General Overview

This strategy is used for students who do poorly on tests. It enables the students to begin preparing at a sufficient time before the test begins.

Steps Used in the Strategy

1. *Day 5.* Have students read the notes they took in class from their textbooks. Also have them read over all the handouts you have provided. Instruct them to highlight, underline, and identify all the important information.
2. *Day 4.* Instruct students to use the techniques they have learned, such as visualization, association, and repetition, to help them remember the important information. Review the notes until all the important information is remembered.
3. *Day 3.* Have students briefly rewrite the important information, using the smallest number of words they can and abbreviations wherever possible. Require students to review their rewritten notes at least twice on this day.
4. *Day 2.* Instruct students to make a list of questions they think will be asked on the test and write answers for these questions.
5. *Day 1.* On the day of the test, allow students to review their rewritten notes from Day 3. Also review the questions and answers prepared on Day 2. Inform students ahead of time that a good time to review is while eating breakfast or while riding to school. Just before the test, instruct students to review anything they are having difficulty remembering.

Additional Information

This strategy will work well for the student who has not yet achieved mastery of what has been taught or who has not had the appropriate assistance.

5.2   BASIS FOR OUTLINING

Desired Outcome

This strategy (Taylor, 1982) leads to improved comprehension and recall of content. Students should be able to write better-organized compositions due to their recognition of details supporting the main idea.

General Overview

This strategy is a hierarchical summary procedure that directs students' attention to how ideas are organized in context. It increases the amount of information students recall after reading. Students' expository compositions usually improve as well. Most middle-grade students learn to use the strategy effectively after eight one-hour sessions.

Steps Used in the Strategy

1. *Previewing.* To begin, have students preview a three- to five-page segment from the text. In forming a skeletal outline, assist students in recording all important information. Use a Roman numeral for each major section in the reading and capital letters for each subsection heading.
2. *Reading and outlining.* Instruct students to read the material subsection-by-subsection. As they read, have them write a summary for each subsection. Help students generate a main idea statement for each subsection (your capital letters) and list supporting details for the main idea.
   a. At the end of each main section, help them create a topic sentence (your Roman numerals).
   b. In the left margin, have the students write phrases for subsections to connect them together.
   c. After doing three hierarchical summaries, encourage students to work with some initial assistance. Finally, they should work independently.
3. *Studying and retelling orally.* After reading the text and writing summaries, have students use the material to study. Have students pair up and retell the other what she has learned. As they take turns, have one student review the summary as the other retells. Encourage partners to help each other with difficult information.

Additional Information

Having students write topic sentences, main idea statements, and supporting details in their own words allows them to reflect on the material.

5.3   CIRCLE OF QUESTIONS

Desired Outcome

Circle of Questions (Sampson, Sampson, & Linek, 1994–1995) engages students in brainstorming, predicting, generating questions about the text, categorizing, and interacting with the text to answer those questions.

General Overview

This strategy was designed as both a prereading and a postreading activity. It is both student- and teacher-directed, promoting critical thinking, cooperative group learning, and research. Circle of Questions lets the readers make their own decisions about what they want to know and provides an outline for them to follow. It also promotes the use of other sources of information to find the answers to students' questions. This strategy can be used with a variety of readers at most elementary levels.

Steps Used in the Strategy

1. Select the topic for learning and the reading material to be used.
2. Arrange students in groups of five and read the given material.
3. Have students determine who will be timekeeper, reporter, recorder, encourager, and an optional leader.
4. Instruct students to brainstorm questions about the topic.
5. Draw a large circle on the board. Write the topic in the center of the circle. Draw several lines coming off the circle and have groups share questions with the class. Record the questions on the board.
6. Review the questions and categorize them.
7. Designate a category in which each group can become an expert.
8. Have students reread the material, searching for the answers to their category questions. Have the recorder write the answers and note where they were found in the reading.
9. Regroup the whole class and have the reporters share their information with the class. Record their answers and sources next to the corresponding questions.
10. Decide as a class if there are any other questions that need to be researched further. If so, repeat the process.

Additional Information

This strategy opens the doorway for many modifications and additional writing activities. It may be helpful to have the students write a few paragraphs about the topic, using their questions and answers as a guide. Also, a mini-library could be set up in the classroom with literature on a specific topic. Students may discover that their textbook is not the only source of information available.

5.4 CSM (CLOZE STORY MAPPING)

Desired Outcome

CSM (Cloze Story Mapping) (Reutzel, 1986) provides students with a framework for organizing, monitoring, and integrating information obtained from either

FIGURE 1 in Strategy 5.3
Circle of Questions

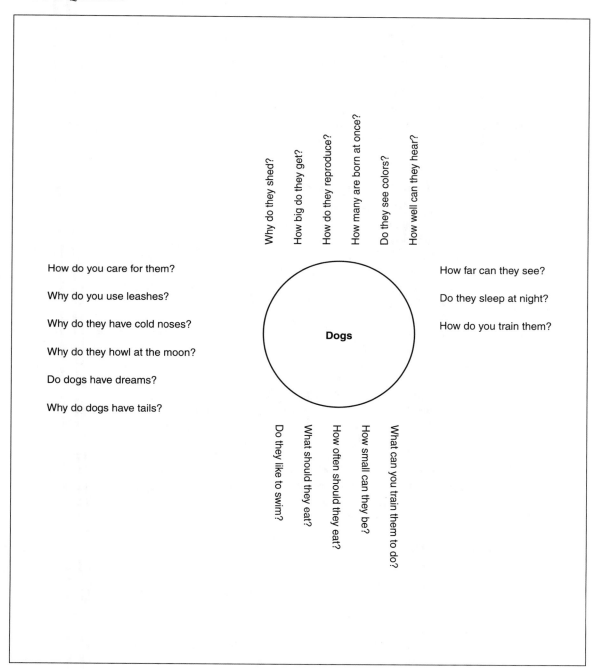

narrative or expository text. Cloze Story Mapping can be used to enhance comprehension before, during, and after reading.

General Overview

Cloze Story Mapping combines the elements of cloze with a story mapping strategy to represent the structure and semantic content of both narrative and expository text. The Cloze Story Map provides structure and enhances comprehension. A framework is provided for organizing, monitoring, and integrating information obtained from text. Students integrate new information into their prior knowledge. Cloze Story Mapping focuses on prediction and the monitoring of comprehension.

Steps Used in the Strategy

Designing a Cloze Story Map

1. Construct a summary list of the main idea, major events, and major characters in the sequence they appear in the text.
2. Place the main idea in a circle or other outline shape in the center of the map.
3. Draw enough ties projecting out from the central shape to handle the major events/characters contained in the summary list. Place these ties symmetrically around the center shape containing the main idea.
4. Center the key words for the major concepts or events in outline shapes attached to the ends of the ties drawn out from the center containing the main idea. Enter the events in sequence, moving clockwise around the center shape.
5. Similarly, enter subevents and subconcepts in a clockwise sequence around the spaces containing major events or concepts.
6. Vary the shapes used to hold the ideas, making the structure of the map easier to perceive. For example, use one shape for major ideas, another for supporting ideas. Use color if you wish.
7. To transform a story map into a Cloze Story Map, move around the shapes, deleting the content of every fifth one (just as in a standard cloze activity). Make all movement around the map clockwise for deletion purposes.
8. Instruct students to complete the Cloze Story Map by filling in the missing shapes with the correct concept or event information.

Using the Cloze Story Map

1. Introduce the story by using an overhead projector to present the Cloze Story Map (CSM) to the whole group.
2. Before reading, have students discuss the story through guided questions related to the CSM and speculate on possible answers for the deleted information.
3. Next, give students a copy of the CSM to help them monitor their comprehension while they read.

4. Encourage students to fill in their CSM as they encounter the deleted information in their reading.
5. After reading, discuss with students the correct information for the deleted information in their CSM.
6. Have the students hand in their CSM, then attempt to fill in another map from memory. After all students have finished, return the completed CSM to students so they can check their reproductions.

Expanding the Cloze Story Mapping Strategy (Before Reading)
1. Engage in predictions about the reading.
2. Logically introduce the story based on the story's structure.
3. Set a discriminating purpose for reading the story.
4. More consciously guide comprehension efforts.
5. Fill in gaps or enhance existing background knowledge of the story.
6. Represent the story's content, using a graphic framework based on the story's inherent semantic relations and the organization of the original text.

Expanding the Cloze Story Mapping Strategy (During Reading)
1. Focus selective attention.
2. Provide periodic checks for comprehension.
3. Structure students' efforts to summarize the story's content.

Expanding the Cloze Story Mapping Strategy (After Reading)
1. Guide the selection and sequence of comprehension review questions.
2. Evaluate comprehension of the story.
3. Study for a test over the content of the story.
   a. Guide the production of a written story summary.
   b. Provide a stimulus for student creations of altered or original Cloze Story Maps.

Additional Information

Cloze Story Mapping can be used to delete major concepts/events and/or subconcepts/subevents only. This strategy is appropriate for elementary through high school students who need help with comprehension or the organization, monitoring, and integration of information.

5.5   COLLABORATIVE LEARNING

Desired Outcome

Collaborative Learning (Jongsma, 1990) is the grouping or pairing of students for the purpose of achieving an academic goal. The grouping creates a social environment with less pressure and academic competition.

FIGURE 1 in Strategy 5.4
Cloze Story Mapping

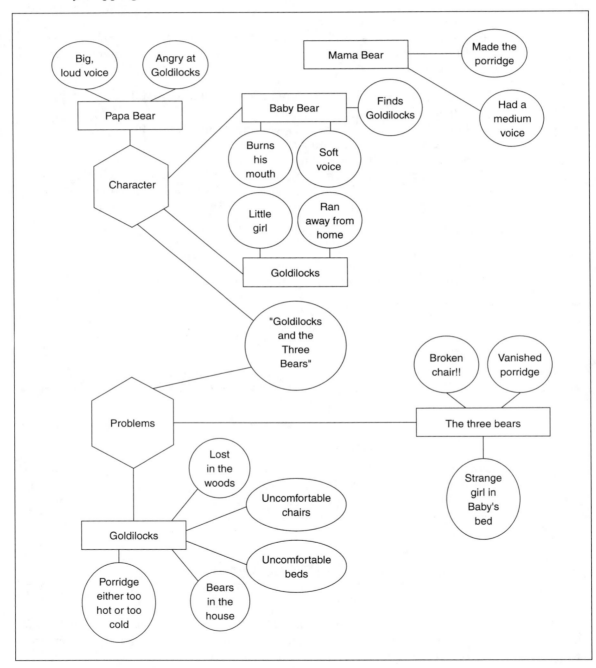

General Overview

This strategy is used to increase self-esteem, decrease dependence on the teacher, achieve higher test scores, give students more positive perceptions about others, and increase the motivation to learn.

Steps Used in the Strategy

For Collaborative Research Activities:

1. Divide students into small groups of about four each.
2. Allow the group members to select the topics they wish to research.
3. Define and narrow the research focus.
4. Encourage group members to brainstorm background knowledge they have about the topic of interest and to work out the formats to share with their classmates.

Additional Information

This activity will work well for undermotivated high school and middle school remedial readers.

5.6   COOPERATIVE GROUP ROTATION

Desired Outcome

Cooperative Group Rotation (Mermelstein, 1994) helps develop reading comprehension and allows students access to a variety of books in a small-group setting. They can participate actively and use information to create projects that demonstrate knowledge about the subject. It also affords students the opportunity to work in a group setting.

General Overview

Cooperative Group Rotation is used as a prereading or during reading activity. Divide students into groups of five. These groups remain stationary as the material being presented by the teacher is passed from group to group. This strategy works best with proficient readers and those who work well in groups.

Steps Used in the Strategy

1. Divide students into groups of approximately five.
2. Assign, or have students assign, jobs at the beginning of each day's session: reader, note taker, and leader. Direct jobs to a different person in the group each day. Have one student act as an assistant if someone needs help.

FIGURE 1 in Strategy 5.5
Collaborative Learning

Vocabulary Word:
Sufficient

Contextual Paragraph
There are cultural disincentives for women to pursue careers in science, technology, and mathematics. Proportionally fewer women and minorities have *sufficient* background for scientific careers—girls take fewer math and science courses in high school, and fewer study scientific subjects in college.

Student Ideas on Possible Meaning

Sufficient: any
             good
             a lot of
             *enough

Similar Situations for Word Use

Sufficient: When you have enough stuff to do something (a *sufficient* amount of materials)

When you are giving someone too much of something (these are *sufficient* for what I am doing—I don't need any more).

When you think you've done enough work (I have spent a *sufficient* amount of time on my homework, so now I will watch TV).

Words with Similar Meanings

    Enough
    Plenty
    Adequate
    Satisfactory

3. Define and discuss jobs with the class before groups meet and set rules for group conduct.
4. Give one book to each group during a session. Choose both fiction and nonfiction books on the subject being taught. Choose the number of books equal to the number of groups formed in the classroom.
5. Instruct students to conduct the activity as follows. The reader reads the book aloud, stopping at the end of each page. The leader should ask, "What do you think was important on that page?" The note taker writes down the group's answers. Spelling is not important at this point.
6. When the group is finished, have each student work on a project about the subject, using the book and notes as resources. Encourage different projects, such as drawing a picture, writing a paragraph, creating an adjective word web, making a puppet, or writing a creative story about the subject.
7. At the next session, rotate the books and have all the groups read each book.
8. Allow each student to choose his best project to display on a large piece of cardboard. Make the projects part of a whole class bulletin board.

Additional Information

As a modification, the students in each group read their book silently. The students also prepare a worksheet with questions about the story that they answer as they read. This could be done to assure comprehension of the story. Students would then, as a group, pick a project to show to the class.

Cooperative Group Rotation can be started as early as second grade and used through middle school. This strategy can be modified for various grade levels and subject areas.

5.7   DIRECTED INQUIRY ACTIVITY

Desired Outcome

This strategy (Lehr, 1980; Thomas, 1978) helps increase reader comprehension in a content area lesson. It aids students in selecting important information and categorizing information from subject area textbooks.

General Overview

The Directed Inquiry Activity aids students in organizing, processing, and comprehending assigned text materials. The use of the six inquiry questions helps them establish a logical base from which to explore both narrative and expository text.

Steps Used in the Strategy

1. Have students preview a section of assigned text.
2. Ask the six inquiry questions (who? what? when? where? why? how?).
3. Record the students' predictions on the board under the appropriate category. Use probing questions and elaboration techniques to get students to remember important information pertaining to the text.
4. Have the students read the assignment and make the necessary changes to their predictions.
5. Use a prereading chart to modify the strategy for use as a pre- and postreading strategy.

Additional Information

This strategy does not allow for introducing vocabulary. Technical terms necessary for students to understand the reading must be provided. Inquiry categories may be eliminated if they are not related to the assigned reading.

5.8 DRTA+SQ (DIRECTED READING THINKING ACTIVITY AND STUDENT QUESTION)

Desired Outcome

This strategy (Smyers, 1987) helps foster independent thinking and improve critical thinking skills through a process involving predictions, reading, and questioning. This strategy also helps students develop good communication skills by giving them practice formulating questions and ideas about the material.

General Overview

The DRTA + SQ (Directed Reading Thinking Activity and Student Question) strategy is a three-step process that includes making predictions, reading, and proving or disproving the predictions based on what was read. By adding the SQ to the strategy, three important things are added: students are involved in the text, boredom is alleviated, and some preparation time is eliminated. DRTA+SQ is a helpful aid when working with both fast and slow readers.

Steps Used in the Strategy

1. Select an exciting story.
2. Mark off three or four points in the story where you can stop reading to allow the students to predict what will occur next in the story.
3. Have the students make initial predictions as to the plot of the story.
4. Have students read to the next stopping point in order to prove or disprove what they have predicted.

FIGURE 1 in Strategy 5.7
Directed Inquiry Activity: *Mariko Goes to Camp* by Judy Delton

Prereading chart

Who	What	When	Where	Why	How
Mariko—a girl Her mom and dad Counselors at camp Some other children Her sisters or brothers	Her trip to camp Things she did at camp How to cook over a fire Cool outdoor games	Summertime For the whole summer For a few weeks For one week	In the woods In the mountains In tents In caves	Her parents wanted to get rid of her. She needed fresh air. Camp was cheaper than a baby-sitter.	They paid money for her to go. Her mom and dad drove her. She took a bus

Postreading Chart

Who	What	When	Where	Why	How
Mariko—a girl Her mom and dad Counselors at camp—Miss Foster Some other children—Julie and Jennifer	Her trip to camp Things she did at camp Fishing Hiking Learning about flowers Roasting marshmallows	Summertime For one week	In the woods In tents	Her mom and dad thought she would have fun and learn to make friends.	She took a bus.

5. At each stopping point, ask the students to write two good questions. Remember to have them include a prediction-eliciting question.
6. Allow each student to ask a question and discuss it with the class.

Additional Information

DRTA+SQ also teaches other important reading skills. It can allow the teacher to model silent reading, neat handwriting, clear questioning, and critical thinking. The teacher can emphasize critical parts of a story, such as plot, character, or setting. The strategy can be used to inspire students to write in complete sentences, and it can motivate slow readers by deemphasizing their reading pace.

5.9 FLIP (FRIENDLINESS, LANGUAGE, INTEREST, PRIOR KNOWLEDGE)

Desired Outcome

The purpose of this strategy (Mangrum & Schumm, 1991) is to enable students to examine their reading assignments and develop an appropriate plan of action for completing them.

General Overview

This strategy is similar to the preview, preread, and overview or survey steps. Students compile a checklist of factors, considering the "friendliness" of text material. Readers must evaluate both text-based and reader-based (prior knowledge) factors to determine the text's level of difficulty.

Steps Used in the Strategy

1. To evaluate the reading assignment, give students FLIP charts to complete.
2. Instruct students to record the title and the number of papers in the assignment, and then begin FLIPping. Rate each of the four elements of FLIP on a scale from 1 to 5, with 5 indicating a positive rating.
3. *F(riendliness).* Have students examine their assignment to locate the friendly text features listed on the FLIP chart.
4. *L(anguage).* Instruct students to skim the assignment to determine the number of new terms. Then have them read three random paragraphs to focus on the vocabulary level and complicated sentences.
5. *I(nterest).* Guide students to read the title, introductions, headings, subheadings, and summary and to examine the pictures and graphics.
6. *P(rior knowledge).* Use the quick survey completed during the Interest step to let the students determine if they have prior knowledge of the assignment subject matter.

7. After all four FLIP elements have been rated, have the students evaluate the overall difficulty of the reading assignment. Have students add up their ratings to get an overall level of comfort for the assignment.

FLIP Follow-up

1. Budget reading time. Have students set mini-goals by "chunking" the assignment or dividing it into manageable parts. Have students read and study one chunk and take a break, then read and study another chunk and take a break, and so on.

Additional Information

This strategy is best suited for high school students and can be used in all curriculum areas, especially content areas.

Students' records of the purpose for reading and students' predictions of text difficulty serve as a guide for reading rate. If the rating is "comfortable" or reading is for personal enjoyment, then the student would read at a faster rate. (Students adjust their rate of reading accordingly.)

5.10   INFORMATION CHARTS

Desired Outcome

Information Charts (Randall, 1996) provide a graphic organizer which helps students learn how to organize material they have collected in a meaningful fashion. They may also use them to ascertain the areas where they need more information, thus improving their questioning and elaboration skills.

General Overview

Information Charts are useful tools when writing any sort of research paper. In this strategy, students are directly instructed to think critically. The structured format provides organization that is critical when dealing with research. Information Charts can be used with grades 4–12 with expository text.

Steps Used in the Strategy

1. Instruct students to select a research topic.
2. Distribute the form for students to complete, indicating their prior knowledge of the subject.
3. Give students time to ascertain what information they need to know and what subtopics to research.
4. Instruct students to find books and articles on those subtopics.

FIGURE 1 in Strategy 5.9
FLIP Strategy

> **Directions:** Examine the assigned story, using the FLIP techniques we have studied. Rate the story in the four FLIP categories, with 1 being the lowest level of difficulty and 5 being the highest. After you have rated each category separately, give the story an overall "friendliness" rating. Then, read the story and decide whether it matched your initial "friendliness" rating.

Name: _____

FLIP Chart for: _____ Mariko Goes to Camp _____

1. **Friendliness.** Are there friendly text features (headings, words in bold print, etc.) in this story?

       1   2   3   4   5

2. **Language.** Are there new and/or difficult words and terms introduced in this story?

       1   2   3   4   5

3. **Interest.** After reading the title, introduction, and subheadings and looking at the pictures, does this look like it will be an interesting story?

       1   2   3   4   5

4. **Prior knowledge.** Do you have any knowledge of the subject or topic this story seems to be about?

       1   2   3   4   5

5. **Overall friendliness rating.** Taking all these factors into consideration, how difficult does this story appear?

       1   2   3   4   5

Postreading Did this story match your perceived friendliness rating? If not, what is your new rating?

       1   2   3   4   5

5. Have students complete the chart with the information they collect.
6. Have students write the paper, using the charts they have completed.

Additional Information

Information Charts are helpful for students who need a structured outline format for writing research papers.

5.11   INTUITIVE READING

Desired Outcome

The purpose of this strategy (Eggar, 1992) is to facilitate better oral reading skills among students. This strategy promotes comprehension and fluency during oral reading.

General Overview

Through relaxation and mental imaging, the student learns to unlock reading strategies that were previously learned and then apply them to oral reading.

Steps Used in the Strategy

1. Instruct students to close their eyes and relax by breathing slowly and deeply while visualizing a color.
2. After relaxing, instruct students to open their eyes slowly and begin to read. This process is done over a long period of time until students get used to the relaxation technique and feel comfortable doing it. If a student hesitates while reading, instruct her to relax and visualize her color again.

Additional Information

This strategy is best suited for older students with a previous knowledge of reading techniques and is appropriate for students who are anxious about reading aloud.

5.12   JOT CHARTS

Desired Outcome

Jot Charts help children become more organized and methodical in their note taking, because they encourage students to focus on the important elements of the

FIGURE 1 in Strategy 5.10

Information Chart

Name: _____	Paper Topic: _____ Sea Creatures _____
What I already know: A lot of different kinds of creatures live in the seas and oceans. Some breathe air and some breathe water. Fish are sea creatures.	

Bibliography #1	Dolphins, whales, sharks, fish, blowfish, snails, porpoises, clams, shrimp
#2	Anemones, scallops, squid, octopus, seals, sea lions, jellyfish, plankton, puffer fish
#3	Sea turtles, sting rays, coral, starfish, crabs, lobsters, mackerel, eels

Interesting related facts: Some whales can grow to weigh more than 40 tons.
Over 3/4 of the Earth's surface is covered by water.
Many sea creatures—such as whales and dolphins—are mammals.
Keywords: Aquatic ecology, marine landscape
New questions to research: What kind of plant life is there in the seas? How do they live deep underwater where the sun doesn't reach?

material. By writing down important concepts, students process the information and are more able to remember it. As students read, they reflect, process, and connect information.

General Overview

In Jot Charts, students develop a simple matrix, the size of which depends on the length and complexity of the reading material. They can be completed during or after reading the material. Jot Charts are particularly helpful when studying for exams, because they help students remember the important elements.

Steps Used in the Strategy

1. Introduce the topic of the upcoming material. Focus on any visuals, such as charts, pictures, diagrams, or maps. The general heading might be the title for the Jot Chart.
2. Have students note the subheadings that can be listed under the general topic. The subheadings should assist students in deciding on subtopics to write in the first column of the Jot Chart.
3. In the remaining columns, have students write down pertinent information about the selected subtopics. One effective procedure is to have students use the subheadings to help them create questions about the important material. These questions can be written in the top of the following column. They give the students direction and a purpose for reading, because they require students to develop their own purpose for reading and to reflect on the information to be covered.
4. Encourage students to read the material to answer the question(s) written at the top of the columns. After reading the answers in the text, have students select keywords and write them in the appropriate columns. Point out to students that complete sentences are inappropriate and that they should avoid including too much detail.

Additional Information

In Jot Charts, it is perhaps most useful to list the main topics to be covered in column one. Alternatives to having questions include listing attributes, characteristics, or details or other characteristics of the main topics in the remaining columns.

5.13 OH RATS (OVERVIEW, HEADINGS, READ, ANSWER, TEST-STUDY)

Desired Outcome

OH RATS (Berrent, 1984) includes reading, selecting relevant information, and reviewing within a workable structure.

FIGURE 1 in Strategy 5.12
Jot Charts

Jot Chart: Sea Creatures

Giant creatures	What size is the creature?	Interesting fact about the creature
Bowhead whale	18 meters long	Its head is 1/3 of its length.
Gray whale	15 meters long	It travels 20,000 kilometers between summer and winter.
Blue whale	30 meters long	It is the largest whale of all and may weight 160 tonnes.

Jot Chart: Inventions

Looking closer	When was it invented?	What was it used for?
Microscope	1590	It was used to study plants.
Telescope	1608	It was used to study the stars.
Endoscope	1956	It was used to see inside the human body.

General Overview

OH RATS stands for Overview, Headings, Read, Answer, Test-Study. This is a note-taking method; therefore, it is appropriate only for students who need to write notes on what has been read.

Steps Used in the Strategy

1. *Step O—Overview.* In order to develop an overview for reading, have the students determine the type of material the upcoming chapter or section will contain. First, instruct students to look at the chapter title and headings and develop an image of what to expect. Have students decide if there is an introduction and summary and read both. At this point, have students mentally make a list of questions that may be answered by the material.
2. *Step H—Headings.* Have students get a notebook used only for this one purpose. At the top of each separate page, have students write the title and page numbers and fold each paper lengthwise. On the left side, have students write several questions for each heading.
3. *Step R—Read.* Allow students to read the selection silently. Don't have students read too lengthy sections at once. Break down the material into something that is manageable for the students. You can have the headings determine the amount students read.
4. *Step A—Answer.* Have students determine the pertinent information and place it in the right column of the folded page. Remind students that this should contain the major points and have students complete this for each of the sections.
5. *Step TS—Test-Study.* Instruct students to use their notes to complete a final review. With their note pages folded in half, have them read the heading questions and try to answer without referring to the right side and their notes. Instruct students to use their notes only if they need to review.

Additional Information

Each step or group of steps should be taught as an independent unit, then as a whole. The students should practice each step separately and in combination. Note taking is a very difficult task, so modeling is very helpful. OH RATS is adaptable, so, after it is learned, the students should modify it to fit their own needs. The students should know that it is an excellent tool for many subjects, but not for all.

5.14   PREVIEWING BOOKS

Desired Outcome

The purpose of this strategy (Graves, Prenn, & Cooke, 1985) is to show children the importance of previewing books, so that they can choose reading material that is appropriate for them.

General Overview

This strategy should be taught to all students at an early age because it helps students select their own reading material without the assistance of the teacher. Otherwise most beginning readers choose material that is much too difficult for them. It allows children to think about themselves, their interests, their reading level, and their motivation for choosing books.

Steps Used in the Strategy

1. Place several books of similar difficulty on a table and allow students to choose a book. At first, guide this process by discussing with the students the title and information in the text. Also, discuss the illustrations and identify characters, special vocabulary, and background information.
2. Ask questions and allow students to make predictions about the outcomes of the plot, which they will clarify during reading. If the book is a mystery, stop previewing before the plot is given away.
3. In the beginning, guide this process. After students are comfortable with previewing, they can do it independently while you serve both as support and as a person to share the excitement of the book with the students. Continue to promote key vocabulary and concepts that may not be evident from the illustrations.

Additional Information

This is an interactive strategy which can be used in large groups, in small groups, and with individual students.

5.15   PSRT (PREPARE, STRUCTURE, READ, AND THINK)

Desired Outcome

This strategy (Langer, 1981; Simons, 1989) teaches both preparation skills and thinking skills, leading to both improved student comprehension of text material and improved critical thinking skills.

General Overview

PSRT (Prepare, Structure, Read, and Think) is a reading comprehension strategy designed for use with subject area lessons that require students to learn from expository textbooks. It activates background knowledge and involves a high level of teacher-pupil interaction. The discussion at the end of the lesson allows the teacher to evaluate literal understanding of the text and encourages the students to think about what they have read.

Steps Used in the Strategy

1. Find out what students already know. First, provide and assess necessary background knowledge. Identify the key concepts of the text and use brainstorming to see what the students already know or have deciphered about the key concept. Record student responses on the chalkboard.
2. Help students understand the text's organization. Prepare a graphic overview of the text. Distribute a blank overview to the students and help them complete the overview with the information they gathered in Step 1.
3. Before expecting students to read the text, set a purpose for reading. Have students read the text independently and complete the rest of the overview.
4. Discuss the text. Call on specific students to complete the chalkboard overview. Ask students to summarize or explain their answers. Discuss the completed overview, asking questions that require the students to think about the text.

Additional Information

This strategy improves comprehension by helping the students recognize the organization of the textbook. The graphic overview is a concrete way to help them understand how the new information in the text links to their existing knowledge. The students can read the passage and fill in the graphic overview as homework or classwork.

5.16 RECIPROCAL TEACHING

Desired Outcome

The purpose of Reciprocal Teaching (Durkin, 1993; Heymsfeld, 1991) is to help students learn how to learn from the text. The teacher and the student take turns being the teacher. There are four common goals: predicting, question generating, summarizing, and clarifying.

General Overview

This strategic process focuses on meaning. It can be used before, during, or after reading. It involves speaking, listening, and reading. By using this strategy, students increase their comprehension and prediction skills, leading to better study skills and comprehension.

Steps Used in the Strategy

1. *Predicting.* To initiate the procedure, make a prediction about the content the students will read silently. Base this prediction on the title of the book or on one paragraph.

2. *Reading.* Read a specified piece of text silently along with the students.
3. *Questioning.* Have whoever is functioning as the teacher pose one or more questions about the passage to be read.
4. *Clarifying.* If any misunderstandings are apparent, clarify them.
5. *Summarizing.* After the questions are answered, have the person acting as the teacher summarize the passages.

Additional Information

This will work with grades 4 through 12. This strategy is helpful for the student who has a history of comprehension difficulty.

5.17   SCAIT (SELECT, COMPLETE, ACCEPT, INFER, AND THINK)

Desired Outcome

This study technique (Wiesendanger & Bader, 1992) helps students select important information in the text related to the lesson's objectives and enables them to develop higher-level thinking skills.

General Overview

The strategy has been used successfully by high school students, primarily for content area subjects. SCAIT stands for *S*—select key words; *C*—complete sentences; *A*—accept final statements; *I*—infer; *T*—think.

Steps Used in the Strategy

1. **S:** *Select key words.* Establish objectives and have students read the material silently and pick out information germane to the lesson's purpose. Have students jot down key words and short, important phrases that relate to prequestions or objectives. (Note the place on each page where the key thought is found for later reference.)
2. **C:** *Complete sentences.* Give strips of paper to the students and have them write one complete sentence on each strip, using keywords and key phrases. Clarify ambiguities by referring to spots marked in the book. Each student selects, elaborates on, and clarifies information before doing group work. Students have time for processing and reacting at their own speed.
3. **A:** *Accept final statements.* Divide the class into cooperative groups of three to five students, each group with high, middle, and low achievers. The group's purpose is (1) to determine if each statement supplied by group members is accurate, (2) to use the text as a verifying source, (3) to eliminate redundant statements, and (4) to eliminate statements not relevant to the lesson objectives.

4. **I:** *Infer.* Students draw inferences from facts. Have groups discuss each written statement and categorize it by the criteria established by the group (determined from studying all statements and noting commonalities). Use two to four categories, depending on the number of pages read and the facts accumulated. The group's main goal is to write general, implied statements on a square piece of paper. Having literal and inferential statements on different shapes of paper (strips vs. squares) helps students remember the distinction.

5. **T:** *Think at the applied level.* In the whole class, have each group articulate the rationale for its selection of literal and inferred statements. This provides an opportunity for students to process important elements of lesson and to compare responses. Discuss each lesson objective separately. Have each group share literal statements for the objective being discussed plus inferential statements derived from them. Use strips of paper to show the relationship among facts and inferences. Have each group leader explain the literal and inferred levels, focusing on how the new information relates to that already learned. As a whole group, develop applied statements that encompass more general ideas. Encourage students to agree or disagree with these; use literal and inferred information to substantiate the general ideas.

Additional Information

SCAIT helps students select important information in the text related to a lesson's objectives and helps them develop the ability to think at inferred and applied levels. The strategy is effective with both expository and narrative text and can easily be implemented at most grade levels. SCAIT involves readers as they determine keywords for a lesson's objectives and statements at both inferred and applied levels. Because the student chooses which information is relevant, SCAIT allows the reader to interact with the material, proceeding from the literal to the interpretive and then back to the literal. This may be important in helping students develop the process necessary to understand the text. Students work both independently and in peer groups.

5.18   THE SCIENTIFIC METHOD

Desired Outcome

The purpose of this strategy (Guerra, 1984) is to increase student comprehension. This activity is effective because it enables the student to activate meaning from the text's material.

General Overview

Students sometimes have difficulty obtaining meaning from the printed page. This strategy encourages students to treat reading as problem solving, relying on rules

SCAIT: Sample High School Social Studies Lesson

The topic was the Middle East. The section of text dealt with characteristics of the land and its relationship to farming. After one class period spent building background and vocabulary, the teacher discussed lesson objectives and wrote them on the board: (1) Determine the conditions of the land and climate in the Middle East. (2) What traits do the people possess? (3) In what ways do the people use their resources?

S: Select key words. Here's a sample list of key words from several students: dry, hilly, melons, oranges, knowledge, irrigate, Nile, farmland, Tigris.

C: Complete sentences. The following are the literal statements composed by the group.

1. Much of the level land in the Middle East and North Africa is too dry for farming, yet this is where farming began thousands of years ago.

2. The land is also too hilly or mountainous to get enough rain for farming.

3. People of the Middle East learned to grow wheat, barley, peas, onions, melons, date palm trees, oranges, and lemons.

4. It takes knowledge, skill, and hard work to grow crops in the dry lands of the Middle East.

5. People in the Middle East irrigate their fields with river water.

6. The Nile River valley is a green strip of irrigated fields and gardens running through the desert.

7. The Middle East and North Africa do not have much good farmland when compared with Europe and North America.

8. Irrigation ditches still carry water from the Tigris and Euphrates rivers over the plain once known as Mesopotamia.

A: Accept final statements. In groups of three, students validated each statement's accuracy and eliminated redundant and nonpertinent ones. (Several statements were redundant, but all were accurate and relevant.)

I: Infer. The group divided the literal statements into three categories: 1, 2, 7—general conditions of the land; 3, 4—resourcefulness of the people; 5, 6, 8—irrigation. The group's task then was to infer a general idea from each group of literal statements and write it on a square piece of paper: from statements 3, 4—the people of the Middle East are skillful, resourceful, intelligent people; from 1, 2, 7—because of the difficult conditions for farming, it is tough to make a living there being a farmer; from 5, 6, 8—people in the Middle East must irrigate their fields from rivers.

T: Think at the applied level. Each group shared its findings in a class discussion and made comparisons with previously learned material or its own experiences. The groups compared the difficulties encountered by Middle Easterners and the Slavs (whom they had studied previously) and ways the two peoples were self-sufficient and used natural resources. The students' next task was to develop general applied statements, taking into account what they had learned about various peoples: (1) people find solutions to many of their problems; (2) humans' desire to survive is strong; and (3) life is better if people cooperate.

or a logical, sequential method. The Scientific Method represents logical thinking, which should be practiced in all areas of study.

Steps Used in the Strategy

1. *Recognize the problem.* Go over the reading's titles and headings. Encourage students to anticipate the meaning of the reading based on titles.
2. *Collect facts.* Help students use brainstorming and other ways to collect facts to activate prior knowledge. These become the basics of knowledge.
3. *Form hypotheses.* Encourage students to use facts to make predictions in the form of questions. Prompt students to think of possible outcomes of their questions in order to remember major points.
4. *Test hypotheses.* Have students read the text and test hypotheses for accuracy and pertinent information. Hold a class discussion to share answers and sort out disagreements by rereading. Remind students that they need to support their positions with material from the text.
5. *Form conclusions.* Instruct students to outline the major points of the assignment and compose a one- or two-paragraph summary of the material. Do this also as a class activity.

Additional Information

Using The Scientific Method, students learn to enhance their reading comprehension. It can help in all content areas as well as narrative text.

5.19 SELECTIVE READING GUIDE-O-RAMA

Desired Outcome

In this strategy (Cunningham & Shablak, 1975), students learn to identify the main idea and the supporting details within a text and incorporate them, as well as other aspects of stories, to create a study guide.

General Overview

In this strategy, the teacher develops a guidance tool for students to use when reading chapters of content textbooks. Students use this as a study guide during their reading to help them understand major ideas and supporting details.

Steps Used in the Strategy

1. Determine a goal and select reading material that the students will need to read. During the planning stage of the strategy, identify the major concepts

and understandings that students should derive from the chapter. Answer
the following questions:
  a. What should students know when they finish the chapter?
    1. What are the major concepts that students should understand?
    2. What supporting information or details should they remember on a
       long-term basis?
  b. What should they be able to do when they finish the chapter?
  c. What background information is essential to perform the required tasks?
  Answering these questions helps identify the essential information within
  the text that you want students to understand. In your textbook margins, you
  can note *M* for main ideas and *D* for the supporting details. You are now
  ready to design the Selective Reading Guide-O-Rama using this information.
2. Present the following ideas:
  a. Pay close attention to this.
  b. Skim over this material.
  c. Read this section carefully.
  d. You can read this section rather quickly, but see if you can find out why.
3. Complete the guide in a logical order. It should move the student from the
   beginning of the chapter through the end.

Additional Information

For students with difficulty handling the written version of the Selective Reading
Guide-O-Rama, a cassette tape version can be made. Students can be cooperatively
grouped to complete the reading, using the Selective Reading Guide-O-Rama and
further discussion. Students who need assistance and who would profit from
structured approaches to develop selective reading skills would benefit from this
strategy, as would students who are frustrated with content area reading and are
overwhelmed with reading assignments.

5.20 SQ3R (SURVEY, QUESTION, READ, RECITE, AND REVIEW)

Desired Outcome

SQ3R is a strategy (Adams, Carnine, & Gersten, 1982; Mangrum & Strichart, 1996;
Scott, 1994; Stahl, King, & Eilers, 1996) involving prediction and elaboration used
to increase literal comprehension and help in the formation of study skills.

General Overview

SQ3R is a strategy that promotes organization, prediction, and comprehension.
Students survey, question, read, recite, and review the material. This strategy improves students' comprehension of textual information and helps them retain the
information for later discussions, quizzes, and tests. This highly structured study

and memory strategy can be used for grades 5–12 and works well with narrative and expository texts.

Steps Used in the Strategy

1. *Survey.* Have students do the following:
   a. Read the title and think about what it means.
   b. Read the introduction, which is usually found in the first paragraph or two.
   c. Read the side headings to learn what the selection is about.
   d. Examine all the visuals and read their captions.
   e. Read the conclusion, which is usually found in the last paragraph or two.
2. *Question.* Have students do the following:
   a. Change the title into one or more questions. Use these keywords to form your questions: *who, what, where, when, why, how.*
   b. Change each side heading into one or more questions. Use these keywords to form your questions: *who, what, where, when, why, how.*
   c. Write the questions.
3. *Read.* Have students do the following:
   a. Read to answer the questions.
   b. Change questions as necessary to answer the questions the author is addressing.
   c. Write answers to the questions to form textbook notes.
4. *Recite.* Have students do the following:
   a. Read the question and its answer aloud.
   b. Read the question aloud; then look away and say the answer aloud.
   c. Read the question aloud; then, with eyes closed, say the answer aloud.
   d. Repeat.
5. *Review* by doing the same things you did for Step 4. Do this once each day for the next three days. Review for more than three days if necessary.

Additional Information

As a modification, add a discussion at the end of the strategy for more comprehension and increased recall of the information. This strategy is appropriate for learning-disabled students as long as the strategy is modeled first. This strategy works well for students with learning disabilities who have difficulty comprehending and retaining the information they read in their textbooks.

5.21   S2RAT (SELECT, REVIEW, RETURN, ASSIGN, AND TEST)

Desired Outcome

S2RAT (Lange, 1983) is a strategy that focuses on improving students' word analysis and word identification skills. Making subject area vocabulary part of the weekly spelling lists increases comprehension due to the repetition.

General Overview

S2RAT incorporates content words from science, social studies, math, and so on into the weekly spelling routine. The students choose the words, thus challenging high-ability students as well as encouraging low-ability students. Activities are done to master the spelling of the content words. This strategy can be used with expository texts for grades 3–12.

Steps Used in the Strategy

1. On Monday, allow students to select 10–25 spelling words from any subject area.
2. On Tuesday, review each student's list of words, checking spelling and appropriateness.
3. Return the lists to the students the same day.
4. On Thursday, have the students use the words to form a list varying in levels of difficulty.
5. Test on Friday. Assign the students a partner of the same ability level. Have students alternate reading the list with their partners.

Additional Information

As a modification to this strategy, a pretest of the spelling words on Wednesday may be added. This way the students can measure their progress and pinpoint words on which they need to concentrate further. This strategy can be used when students are having difficulty grasping the meanings of content words. It can also be used when studying a subject with difficult, but meaningful, vocabulary.

5.22 TEXT PREVIEW

Desired Outcome

The desired outcome of this strategy (McKenzie, Smith, Hubler, Ericson, & Bean, 1987) is to build students' knowledge of a selection prior to reading, thus contributing to comprehension at and beyond the literal level.

General Overview

Text Preview is a prereading exercise to provide students with a detailed framework for comprehending a selection.

Steps Used in the Strategy

1. Initiate an interest building session, such as a discussion or a related activity. Use several statements and questions which connect the major topics and issues within the text with experiences familiar to the student.

2. Instruct students to write a synopsis which describes setting, characters, point of view, tone, key elements of the plot (excluding the outcome), and theme.
3. After reading, have students review the main characters and give definitions of important vocabulary. To aid in this process, pose several questions for guiding the students' reading.

Additional Information

Previews should be at least 400 words long, but consider the ability and age level of the students.

5.23   TEXT STRUCTURE

Desired Outcome

The purpose of this strategy (Vacca & Vacca, 1989) is to increase comprehension by helping students understand the way texts are structured.

General Overview

The Text Structure strategy is designed to help students recognize and use expository text structures to understand better and recall informational texts. It is based on the premise that, if students are taught different expository structures, they can use an understanding of these structures as an aid in comprehending texts that have a similar structure. Using a particular text structure when writing demonstrates understanding of the usefulness of this strategy.

Steps Used in the Strategy

Steps Used by the Teacher

1. Learn about text structure and analyze the structure of the expository material you are using. The following are the three main text structures:
   a. A *causative text structure* is one in which a relationship is specified between reasons and results in a time sequence.
   b. A *problem/solution structure* is similar to a causative structure, except that a solution is added to the structure that is designed to break the causative link.
   c. A *comparative structure* organizes elements on the basis of their similarities and differences and implies no causality or time sequence.
2. Select expository text that is well organized and consists of a predominant structure.
3. Actively involve students in the reading of the text and the discussion afterward.

FIGURE 1 in Strategy 5.22
Text Preview: *Little Women*

Setting	Characters	Tone
During and following the Civil War The March home and the town they live in—a small New England town.	The March girls—Meg, Jo, Beth, and Amy Their mother and father Mr. Laurence and Laurie, his grandson	Hopeful Emphasis on family
Point of View	**Plot Elements**	**Theme**
Written by an outside narrator Focus is mainly on Jo	The family must get along while Father is at war. The sisters sometimes fight. They have fun and adventures with Laurie. They slowly grow up.	Family ties are the most important, and it is better to help others than to help yourself.

Steps Used in the Instruction

1. *Modeling.* Before expecting students to use text structure, it is necessary to demonstrate what it is. Model the thought processes, focusing on text structure knowledge. Use think-alouds. Use passages that students will encounter in their reading, since these are the most relevant for students. During modeling, it is essential to show students a particular text structure and point out why it is a certain type and how that type is organized. It is also important to point out any words that signal or cue the text structure. For example, point out words such as *however, because,* and *therefore.*

2. *Recognition.* Walk through a particular text structure with the students. This can be done on a listening level with students before reading. Place the attention on listening and deciding on text structure, rather than on reading. Also, focus on sentences or paragraphs before moving on to lengthier passages. The essential thing is to have students verbalize the why and how of the text structure. Use a checklist as a guide to help students recognize text structure.

5.24   UNDERLINING

Desired Outcome

The desired outcome of the Underlining strategy is to improve prediction, comprehension, and organization while reading.

General Overview

This is an organizational strategy used by mature, effective readers to identify unique words, phrases, or figures of speech that will affect their comprehension of a particular selection. It can be used before, during, and after reading, and it is best implemented using an expository text or a short narrative story.

Steps Used in the Strategy

1. Select a passage of 100 to 150 words from the beginning of a short story or chapter in a text.
2. Underline five to seven words or phrases that are key concepts.
3. Hand out copies of the passage already underlined and read the passage aloud, discussing as a group why each key concept is underlined.
4. Using these key concepts, have the students predict the content of the rest of the story/chapter.
5. Give students the original source (the rest of the story/chapter) and encourage them to underline what they feel is important for the remaining paragraphs.
6. Allow students to discuss their choices, to comment on their choices, and to decide if more practice with underlining is necessary. Students can use their underlining skills as a study technique and/or for review of material.

Additional Information

This is an appropriate strategy for students who are experiencing difficulty with study skills. This strategy emphasizes what the key concepts are in a passage and highlights them using underlining. With practice, those students feeling overwhelmed while studying will soon learn to study only those important facts.

5.25   WAGON WHEELS

Desired Outcome

The purpose of this strategy (Feddersen, 1988) is to serve as a visual aid to help students organize their thoughts and perceptions of a piece of text. This strategy improves students' organizational and concept analysis skills.

General Overview

The Wagon Wheels strategy is a helpful graphic organizer used to aid students in what they already know and what they must find out in the material. It answers the *who, what, when, where, why,* and *how* questions pertaining to a particular concept. The Wagon Wheel can be used when studying stories, religion, science, and vocabulary, when writing reports, or when describing personal experiences.

Steps Used in Strategy

1. Draw a Wagon Wheel and write the concept in the hub.
2. Make six spokes coming out of the hub.
3. Put *who, what, when, where, why,* and *how* on each spoke.
4. Draw another circle at the end of each spoke to contain the relevant data answering each question.
5. Have the students read the material, then fill in the circles, completing the wheel.
6. Discuss with the students.

Additional Information

This strategy is a creative and helpful graphic organizer. It can be used as a preview, a study guide, and as a review of the concept. The students can develop a better understanding and write more thoroughly about the topic with the Wagon Wheels aid. Once they have become familiar with the strategy, they can keep the model in mind while reading and can organize the material mentally.

FIGURE 1 in Strategy 5.25
Wagon Wheels: The Jungle

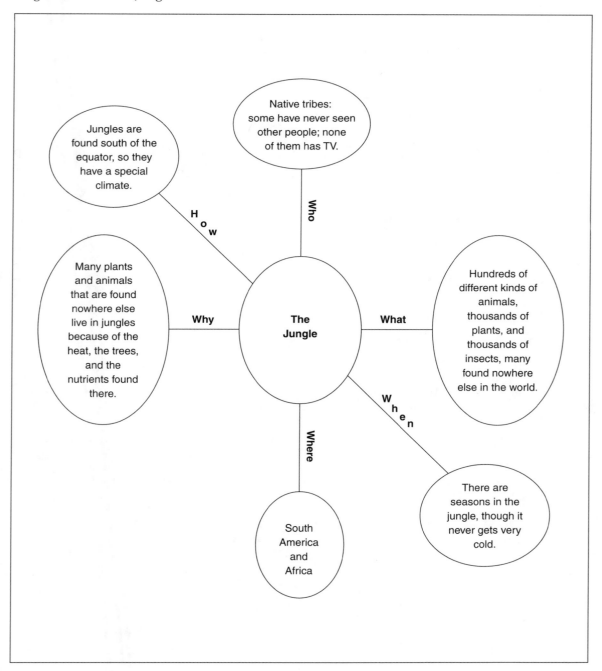

References

Adams, A., Carnine, D., & Gersten, R. (1982). Instructional strategies for studying content area texts in the intermediate grades. *Reading Research Quarterly, 18*, 27–55.

Afflerbach, P., & Walker, B. (1990). Prediction instruction in basal readers. *Reading Research and Instruction, 29*, 25–45.

Allington, R., Stuetzel, H., Shake, M., & Lamarche, S. (1986). What is remedial reading: A descriptive study. *Reading Research and Instruction, 25*, 15–20.

Alverman, D. (1996). Peer-led discussions: Whose interests are served? *Journal of Adolescent and Adult Literacy, 39*, 282–289.

Anders, P., & Bos, C. (1986). Semantic feature analysis: An interactive strategy for vocabulary development and text comprehension. *Journal of Reading, 29*, 610–616.

Anderson, B., & Barnitz, J. (1984). Cross-cultural schemata and reading comprehension instruction. *Journal of Reading, 27*, 102–107.

Banwart, B., & Duffelmeyer, F. (1993). Word maps for adjectives and verbs. *The Reading Teacher, 46*(4), 351–353.

Baumann, J., Jones, L., & Seifert-Kesel, N. (1993). Using think alouds to enhance children's comprehension monitoring abilities.*The Reading Teacher, 47*(3), 184–193.

Beentjes, J., & Van Der Voort, T. (1988). Television's impact on children's reading skills: A review of research. *Reading Research Quarterly, 23*, 389–413.

Bergenske, D. M. (1987). The missing link in narrative story mapping. *The Reading Teacher, 41*(3), 333–335.

Berrent, H. (1984). OH RATS—A note-taking technique. *Journal of Reading, 27*(6), 548–550.

Birkmire, D. (1985). Text processing: The influence of text structure, background knowledge, and purpose. *Reading Research Quarterly, 20*, 314–326.

Blachowicz, C. (1986). Making connections: Alternatives to the vocabulary notebook. *Journal of Reading, 29*, 643–649.

Bligh, T. (1995). Using story impressions to improve comprehension. *Reading Horizons, 35*(4), 287–296.

Bridge, C., Belmore, S., Moskow, S., Cohen, S., & Matthews, P. (1984). Topicalization and memory for main ideas in prose. *Journal of Reading Behavior, 16*, 61–80.

Bromley, K. (1989). Buddy journals make the reading-writing connection. *The Reading Teacher, 43*(2), 122–129.

Bromley, K., Schlimmer, K., & Winters, D. (1994). Buddies: Creating enthusiasm for literacy learning. *The Reading Teacher, 47*(5), 392–399.

Carbo, M. (1978). Teaching reading with talking books. *The Reading Teacher, 32*(3), 267–273.

Carr, E., Dewitz, P., & Patberg, J. (1989). Using cloze for inference training with expository text. *The Reading Teacher, 42*(6), 380–385.

Carr, E., & Ogle, D. (1987). KWL Plus: A strategy for comprehension and summarization. *Journal of Reading, 30*, 626–631.

Casale, U. (1985). Motor imaging: A reading-vocabulary strategy. *Journal of Reading, 28*, 619–621.

Castle, K. (1990). Children's invented games. *Childhood Education, 67*, 82–85.

Chomsky, C. (1976). After decoding: What? *Language Arts, 53*, 288–296.

Chou-Hare, V., & Pulliam, C. (1980). Teacher questioning: A verification and extension. *Journal of Reading Behavior, 12*, 69–72.

Clay, M. (1991). Introducing a new storybook to young readers. *The Reading Teacher, 45*, 264–273.

Clewell, S. F., & Haidemos, J. (1983). Organizational strategies to increase comprehension. *Reading World, 22*(4), 314–321.

Crist, B. (1975). One capsule a week: A painless remedy for vocabulary ills. *Journal of Reading, 19*(2), 147–149.

Crowley, J. (1991). Joy of Big Books. *The Reading Teacher, 45*(9), 743–744.

Cudd, E., & Roberts, L. (1987). Using story frames to develop reading comprehension in a 1st grade classroom. *The Reading Teacher, 41*(1), 75–79.

Cunningham, D., & Shablak, S. (1975). Selective reading guide-o-rama: The content teacher's best friend. *Journal of Reading, 18*, 380–382.

Cunningham, J. W., Cunningham, P. M., & Arthur, S. V. (1981). *Middle and secondary school reading*. New York: Longman.

Cunningham, P. (1979). Imitative reading. *The Reading Teacher, 33*, 80–83.

Cunningham, P., & Cunningham, J. (1992). Making words: Enhancing the invented spelling-decoding connection. *The Reading Teacher, 46*(2), 106–115.

Cunningham, P., Hall, D., & Defee, M. (1991). Non-ability grouped, multilevel instruction: A year in a first-grade classroom. *The Reading Teacher, 44*, 556–571.

Dana, C., & Rodriguez, M. (1992). TOAST: A system to study vocabulary. *Reading Research and Instruction, 31*(4), 78–84.

Davis, Z. T., & McPherson, M. D. (1989). Story map instruction: A road map for reading comprehension. *The Reading Teacher, 43*(3), 232–240.

Dowhower, S. (1989). Repeated reading: Research into practice. *The Reading Teacher, 42*, 502–507.

Duncan, P. (1993). I liked the book better: Comparing film and text to build critical comprehension. *The Reading Teacher, 46*(8), 720–725.

Durkin, D. (1993). *Teaching them to read.* Needham Heights, MA: Allyn and Bacon.

Dynak, J. (1996). Structuring literacy course tasks to foster deliberate use of strategy instruction by preservice math teachers. *Journal of Adolescent and Adult Literacy, 40*(4), 280–285.

Eggar, L. (1992). Unlocking the mind for reading. *Journal of Reading, 35*(8), 658–659.

Ehri, L., & Robbins, C. (1992). Beginners need some decoding skills to read words by analogy. *Reading Research Quarterly, 27*, 12–26.

Elliot, I. (1991). The reading place. *Teaching Pre K-8, 22*(3), 30–34.

Erickson, B. (1996). Read-alouds reluctant readers relish. *Journal of Adolescent and Adult Literacy, 40*(3), 212–214.

Erickson, B., Hubler, M., Bean, T., Smith, C., & McKenzie, J. (1987). Increasing critical thinking in junior high classrooms. *Journal of Reading, 30*, 430–439.

Feddersen, C. (1988). Wagon wheels and writing. *The Reading Teacher, 41*(4), 490–491.

Fitzgerald, J. (1983). Helping readers gain self-control over reading comprehension.*The Reading Teacher, 37*, 249–253.

Fitzpatrick, R. (1994). Cross-age interaction builds enthusiasm for reading and writing. *The Reading Teacher, 47*(4), 292–300.

Flatley, J., & Rutland, A. (1986). Using wordless picture books to teach linguistically/culturally different students. *The Reading Teacher, 40*(3), 276–281.

Flood, J., & Lapp, D. (1988). Conceptual mapping strategies for understanding information texts. *The Reading Teacher, 41*(8), 780–783.

Floriani, B. (1989). Word expansions for multiplying sight vocabulary. *The Reading Teacher, 33*(2), 155–156.

Fowler, G. (1982). Developing comprehension skills in primary students through the use of story frames. *The Reading Teacher, 37*, 176–179.

Galda, L. (1982). Playing about a story: Its impact on comprehension. *The Reading Teacher, 36*, 52–58.

Gambrell, L., & Koskinen, P. (1993). Captioned video and vocabulary: An innovative practice in literacy instruction. *The Reading Teacher, 47*(1), 36–42.

Gammage, S. (1993). Elaboration: Strong and simple. *The Reading Teacher, 46*(5), 446–447.

Gee, T., & Olsen, M. (1991). Content reading instruction in the primary grades: Perception and strategies. *The Reading Teacher, 45*(4), 298–306.

Goldman, M., & Goldman, S. (1988). Reading with closed-captioned television. *Journal of Reading, 31*, 458–461.

Goodman, Y. (1996). Revolving readers while readers revolve themselves: Retrospective miscue analysis. *The Reading Teacher, 49*(8), 600–609.

Goswami, U., & Mead, F. (1992). Onset and rime awareness and analogies in reading. *Reading Research Quarterly, 27*, 153–162.

Graves, D., Prenn, M., & Cooke, C. (1985). The coming attraction: Previewing short stories. *Journal of Reading, 28*, 594–598.

Greenwood, S. (1988). How to use analogy instruction to reinforce vocabulary. *Middle School Journal, 19*(2), 11–13.

Greenwood, S., & Hoffbenkoske, K. (1995). The use of word analogy instruction with developing readers. *The Reading Teacher, 48*(5), 446–447.

Guerra, C. (1984). The scientific method helps secondary students read their textbooks. *Journal of Reading, 27*(6), 487–489.

Gunning, T. (1995). Word building: A strategic approach to the teaching of phonics. *The Reading Teacher, 48*(6), 484–488.

Haggard, M. (1986). The vocabulary self-collection strategy: Using student interest and world knowledge to enhance vocabulary growth. *Journal of Reading, 29*, 634–642.

Haggard, M. (1988). Developing critical thinking with the directed reading thinking activity. *The Reading Teacher, 41*(6), 526–533.

Hansen, J., & Pearson, P. (1983). An instructional study: Improving the inferential comprehension of good and poor fourth-grade readers. *Journal of Educational Psychology, 75*, 821–829.

Harrington, S. (1994). An author's storyboard technique as a pre-writing strategy. *The Reading Teacher, 48*(3), 283–286.

Heller, M. (1986). How do you know what you know? Metacognitive modeling in the content areas. *Journal of Reading, 29*, 415–422.

Herrmann, B. (1992). Teaching and assessing strategic reasoning: Dealing with the dilemmas. *The Reading Teacher, 45*(6), 428–433.

Heymsfeld, C. (1991). Reciprocal teaching. *The Reading Teacher, 45*(9), 335.

Higdon, P. (1987). Sticker books sight words. *The Reading Teacher, 41*(3), 369.

Higginson, B., & Phelan, P. (1986). Word cluster: A strategy for synonym development. *Reading Horizons, 26*(3), 174–178.

Hilbert, S. (1992). Sustained Silent Reading revisited. *The Reading Teacher, 46*, 354–356.

Johnson, B., & Lehnert, L. (1984). Learning phonics naturally: A model for instruction. *Reading Horizons, 24*(2), 90–98.

Jolly, H., Jr. (1981). Teaching basic function words. *The Reading Teacher, 35*(2), 136–140.

Jongsma, K. (1990). Collaborative learning. *The Reading Teacher, 43,* 346–347.

Juel, C. (1991). Cross-age tutoring between student athletes and at-risk children. *The Reading Teacher, 45,* 178–186.

Kapinus, B., & Stahl, S. (1991). Possible sentences: Predicting word meaning to teach content area vocabulary. *The Reading Teacher, 45*(1), 36–43.

Klemp, R. M. (1994). Word Storm: Connecting vocabulary to the student's database. *The Reading Teacher, 48*(3), 282.

Konopak, B., & Williams, N. (1988). Using the keyword method to help young readers learn content material.*The Reading Teacher, 41*(7), 682–687.

Koskinen, P., & Blum, I. (1986). Paired repeated reading: A classroom strategy for developing fluent reading. *The Reading Teacher, 40*(1), 70–75.

Kreeft, J. (1984). Dialogue writing: Bridge from talk to essay writing. *Language Arts, 61,* 141–150.

Lange, J. (1983). Using S2RAT to improve reading skills in the content areas. *The Reading Teacher, 36*(4), 402–404.

Langer, J. (1981). From theory to practice: A prereading plan. *Journal of Reading, 25,* 152–156.

Lehr, F. (1980). Content area reading instruction in the elementary school. *The Reading Teacher 33*(7), 888–891.

Levenson, S. (1979). Teaching reading and writing to limited and non English speakers in secondary schools. *The English Journal, 68,* 38–43.

Levesque, J. (1989). ELVES: A read-aloud strategy to develop listening comprehension. *The Reading Teacher, 43*(1), 93–94.

Lewkowicz, N. (1994). The bag game: An activity to heighten phonemic awareness. *The Reading Teacher, 47*(6), 508–509.

Lombard, M. (1989). ReQuest a fact. *The Reading Teacher, 42*(7), 548.

Mandeville, T. (1994). KWLA: Linking the affective and cognitive domains. *The Reading Teacher, 47*(8), 679–680.

Mangrum, C., & Schumm J. (1991). FLIP: A framework for content area reading. *Journal of Reading, 35*(2), 120–124.

Mangrum II, C. T., & Strichart, S. S. (1993). *Teaching Study Strategies to Students With Learning Disabilities.* Boston: Allyn and Bacon.

Manning, M., & Manning, G. (1995). Reading and writing in the content areas. *Teaching Pre K-8, 26*(1), 152–153.

Manzo, A. V. (1968). The ReQuest procedure. *Journal of Reading, 12,* 123–126.

Manzo, A. V. (1975). Guided reading procedure. *Journal of Reading, 18,* 287–291.

Matter, E. (1989). Visualize to improve comprehension. *The Reading Teacher, 42* (4), 338.

McCauley, J., & McCauley, D. (1992). Using choral reading to promote language learning for ESL students. *The Reading Teacher, 45*(7), 526–533.

McCutchen, D., Bell, L. D., France, I. M., & Perfetti, C. A. (1991). Phoneme-specific interference in reading: The tongue-twister effect revisited. *Reading Research Quarterly, 26,* 87–103.

McKenzie, J. V., Smith, C. C., Hubler, M., Ericson, B., & Bean, T. W. (1987). Increasing critical reading in junior high classrooms. *Journal of Reading, 40*(8), 430–439.

McLaughlin, E. M. (1987). QUIP: A writing strategy to improve comprehension of expository structure. *The Reading Teacher, 40*(7), 650–654.

Mermelstein, B. (1994). Cooperative group rotation. *The Reading Teacher, 48*(3), 281–282.

Morris, D., & Nelson, L. (1992). Supported oral reading with low-achieving second graders. *Reading Research and Instruction, 31,* 49–63.

Mulhall, M. (1992). Kinderjournals.*The Reading Teacher, 45,* 738–739.

Norton, D. (1992). Engaging children in literature: Modeling inferencing of characterization. *The Reading Teacher, 46,* 64–67.

Ogle, D. (1986). K-W-L: A teaching model that develops active reading of expository text. *The Reading Teacher, 39*(6), 564–568.

Pearson, P. (1985). Changing the face of reading comprehension instruction. *The Reading Teacher, 38,* 724–737.

Perrone, V. (1994). How to engage students in learning. *Educational Leadership, 48*(1), 11–13.

Pointdexter, C. (1995). Applying effective reading techniques in content area classes. *Reading Horizons, 35*(3), 244–249.

Randall, S. (1996). Information charts: A strategy for organizing student research. *Journal of Adolescent & Adult Literacy, 39*(7), 536–542.

Raphael, T. (1982). Question-answering strategies for children. *The Reading Teacher, 36,* 186–190.

Reutzel, D. (1986). Clozing in on comprehension: The Cloze Story Map. *The Reading Teacher, 39*(6), 524–528.

Reutzel, D., & Hollingsworth, P. (1988). Highlighting key vocabulary: A generative-reciprocal procedure for teaching selected inference types. *Reading Research Quarterly, 23,* 358–378.

Richards, J., & Gipe, J. (1993). Getting to know story characters: A strategy for young and at-risk readers. *The Reading Teacher, 47*(1), 78–79.

Richards, J., Gipe, J., & Necaise, M. (1994). Find the features and connect them. *The Reading Teacher, 48*(2), 187–188.

Richards, K. (1993). Using semantic mapping, cooperative groups, and toys to build descriptive writing.*The Reading Teacher, 46*(5), 449–450.

Richek, M., & McTague, B. (1988). The "Curious George" strategy for students with reading problems. *The Reading Teacher, 42*(3), 220–226.

Riley, J. (1986). Progressive cloze as a remedial technique. *The Reading Teacher, 39*(6), 576–581.

Robb, L. (1996). Use predictions to help kids think deeply about books: The prediction book report. *Instructor, 106*(3), 61.

Robb, L. (1997a). Building phonics and vocabulary skills through word study: Thematic word wall. *Instructor, 106*(5), 26.

Robb, L. (1997b). Visualize the story to help students comprehend: Double-entry reading journals. *Instructor, 106*(6), 46.

Robb, L. (1997c). Visualize the story to help students comprehend: Informal books. *Instructor, 106*(6), 47.

Roderick, J., & Berman, L. (1984). Dialoguing about dialogue journals. *Language Arts,* Vol. 61, No. 7 686–692.

Sampson, M. B., Sampson, M. R., & Linek, W. (1994–1995). Circle of questions. *The Reading Teacher, 48*(4), 364–365.

Sandberg, K. (1981). Learning to read history actively. *Journal of Reading, 25,* 158–160.

Schwartz, R., & Raphael, T. (1985). Concept of definition: A key to improving students' vocabulary. *The Reading Teacher, 39*(2), 198–205.

Scott, J. (1994). Teaching nonfiction with the shared book experience. *The Reading Teacher, 47*(8), 676–678.

Shanahan, T., Robinson, B., & Schneider, M. (1995). Avoiding some of the pitfalls of thematic units. *The Reading Teacher, 48*(4), 350–353.

Sharp, D. (1991). Effective use of diagrams. *The Reading Teacher, 45*(2), 162–164.

Shoop, M. (1986). InQuest: A listening and reading comprehension strategy. *The Reading Teacher, 39*(7), 670–674.

Silkebakken, G., & Camp, D. (1993). A five-step strategy for teaching analogous reasoning to middle school students. *Middle School Journal, 24*(4), 47–50.

Simons, S. (1989). PSRT—A reading comprehension strategy. *Journal of Reading, 32*(5), 419–426.

Smith, H. M., & Reed, D. (1982). Teaching visual literacy through wordless picture books. *The Reading Teacher, 35*(8), 928–933.

Smith, S. (1985). Comprehension and comprehension monitoring by experienced readers. *Journal of Reading, 28,* 292–300.

Smyers, T. (1987). Add SQ to the DRTA-write. *The Reading Teacher, 41*(3), 372–374.

Sorrell, A. (1990). Three reading strategies: TELLS, story mapping, and QARs. *Academic Therapy, 25*(3), 359–368.

Speaker, R. (1991). Sentence collecting: Authentic literacy events in the classroom. *Journal of Reading, 35*(2), 92–95.

Spiegel, D. (1980). Adaptions of Manzo's guided reading procedure. *Reading Horizons, 20,* 188–192.

Stahl, N., King, J., & Eilers, U. (1996). Post secondary reading strategies rediscovered. *Journal of Adolescent & Adult Literacy, 39*(5), 368–378.

Stanovich, K. (1986). Matthew effects in reading: Some consequences of individual differences in the acquisition of literacy. *Reading Research Quarterly, 41,* 360–407.

Stark, C. (1987). A story writing map. *The Reading Teacher, 40*(9), 926–927.

Stauffer, R. G. (1969). *Directing reading maturity as a cognitive process.* New York: Harper and Row.

Stewart, R., & Cross, T. (1991). The effect of marginal glosses on reading comprehension and retention. *Journal of Reading, 35*(1), 4–11.

Surbeck, E., & Glover, M. (1992). Seal revenge: Ecology games invented by children. *Childhood Education, 68,* 275–281.

Swan, A. (1992). Wordless picture book buddies. *The Reading Teacher, 45*(8), 655.

Taylor, B. (1982). A summarizing strategy to improve middle grade students' reading and writing skills. *The Reading Teacher, 36*(2), 202–204.

Taylor, B., & Beach, R. (1984). The effects of text structure instruction on middle-grade students' comprehension and production of expository text. *Reading Research Quarterly, 19,* 134–146.

Thomas, K. (1978). The directed inquiry activity: An instructional procedure for content reading. *Reading Improvement, 15*(2), 138–140.

Tipton, J. (1991). Extending context clues to composition and cooperative learning. *Journal of Reading, 35,* 50.

Vacca, R., & Padak, N. (1990). Who is at risk in reading? *Journal of Reading, 33,* 486–488.

Vacca, R., & Vacca, J. (1989). *Content area reading.* Glenview, IL: Scott, Foresman.

Weissman, K. (1996). Using paragraph frames to complete a KWL. *The Reading Teacher, 50*(3), 271–272.

Wiesendanger, K., & Bader, L. (1992). SCAIT: A study technique to develop students' higher comprehension skills when reading content area material. *Journal of Reading, 35*(5), 399–400.

Wolf, K., & Siu-Runyan, Y. (1996). Portfolio purposes and possibilities. *Journal of Adolescent and Adult Literacy, 40*(1), 30–36.

Wood, K. (1984). Probable passages: A writing strategy. *The Reading Teacher, 37*(6), 496–499.

Wood, K., & Mateja, J. (1983). Adapting secondary-level strategies for use in elementary classrooms. *The Reading Teacher, 36*(6), 492–496.

Wood, K., & Robinson, N. (1983). Vocabulary, language and prediction: A prereading strategy. *The Reading Teacher, 36*(4), 392–395.

Worthy, M. J., & Bloodgood, J. W. (1993). Enhancing reading instruction through Cinderella tales. *The Reading Teacher, 46,* 290–301.

Yopp, H. (1992). Developing phonemic awareness in young children. *The Reading Teacher, 45*(9), 696–703.

Zutell, J. (1996). The directed spelling thinking activity (DSTA): Providing an effective balance in word study instruction. *The Reading Teacher, 50*(2), 98–108.

Index

Adams, A., 194
Adjective/verb/noun maps (strategy), 44–45, 46–48
Afflerbach, P., 122
Alverman, D., 85
Anders, P., 68
Anderson, B., 60
Anticipation guide (strategy), 78–79, 80–81
Arthur, S.V., 56

Background knowledge, 75
Bader, L., 190
Bag game (strategy), 8
Banwart, B., 44
Barnitz, J., 60
Base, 14
Basic function word(s) (strategy), 9–10, 11, 12
Basis for outlining (strategy), 168–169
Baumann, J., 134
Beach, R., 50
Bean, T., 78
Bean, T.W., 196
Beentjes, J., 79
Beginning readers, 23, 35, 40, 151
Bell, L.D., 24
Belmore, S., 155
Bergenske, D.M., 130
Berman, L., 141
Berrent, H., 185
Big books (strategy), 45
Birkmire, D., 155
Blachowicz, C., 65
Blend, 14, 15, 21, 25
Blending phonemes, 21, 25
Bligh, T., 122
Bloodgood, J.W., 127
Blum, I., 17

Bos, C., 68
Bridge, C., 155
Bromley, K., 136, 141
Buddy journals (strategy), 141–142

Capsules (strategy), 49
Captioned video (strategy), 79
Carbo, M., 9, 25
Carnine, D., 194
Carr, E., 50, 99
Casale, U., 64
Castle, K., 91
Character analysis (strategy), 82, 83
Charts (strategies)
    compare and contrast, 6, 52, 180, 181, 183, 185, 186
    information, 181, 183, 184
    jot, 183, 185
    KWL, 100, 103
    semantic feature analysis, 68, 71, 72–74
Chomsky, C., 25
Choral reading (strategy), 82, 84
Chou-Hare, V., 108
Circle of questions (strategy), 169–170, 171
Clay, M., 122
Clewell, S.F., 107
Cloze
    instruction (strategy), 50, 51
    story map (strategy), 170, 172–173, 174
Cluster, 15, 37
Cohen, S., 155
Collaborative learning (strategy), 173, 175, 176
Comprehending, 64, 79, 99
Comprehension, 11, 19, 27, 31, 35, 50, 57, 58, 61, 63, 64, 66, 67, 79, 82, 84,

85, 86, 91, 94, 97, 98, 99, 100, 104, 105, 107, 111, 112, 113, 114, 116, 124, 126, 127, 131, 134, 135, 136, 149, 154, 168, 172, 175, 177, 183, 188, 189, 191, 194, 196, 197, 199
Conceptual mapping (strategy), 50, 52, 53–55
Connecting words, 9
Consonant
    blends, 15
    clusters, 15
    digraphs, 15
    sounds, 8, 15
Content area material, 177, 181, 194
Context clues, 21, 23, 52, 56, 65
Contextual
    processing (strategy), 52
    redefinition (strategy), 56–47
Cooke, C., 187
Cooperative group rotation (strategy), 175, 177
Creating an animated film (strategy), 84–85
Crist, B., 49
Cross, T., 63
Crowley, J., 45
Cudd, E., 124
Cue, 25, 50
Cunningham, D., 94, 193
Cunningham, J.W., 56
Cunningham, P., 9
Cunningham, P.M., 56
Curious George (strategy), 142–143

Dana, C., 71
Davis, Z.T., 88
Decode, 15, 24, 35
Decoding, 16, 24, 34, 35
Dewitz, P., 50

Digraph
 consonant, 15
 vowel, 15
Directed inquiry activity (strategy), 177–178, 179
Discussion web (strategy), 85–86, 87
Double-entry reading journal (strategy), 144, 145
Dowhower, S., 112
DRTA (strategy), 86, 88
DRTA + SQ (strategy), 178, 180
DSTA (strategy), 10, 13
Duffelmeyer, F., 44
Duncan, P., 82, 84, 157
Durkin, D., 13, 189
Dynak, J., 131

Eggar, L.,183
Ehri, L., 34
Eilers, U., 194
Elaboration (strategy), 144, 146
Elliot, I., 111
ELVES (strategy), 57–58
Episodic mapping (strategy), 88–90
Erickson, B., 78, 111, 196
Every pupil response, 17

Fedderson, C., 200
Find the features (strategy), 91–92
Fitzgerald, J., 98
Fitzpatrick, R., 17
Five-Day test preparation plan (strategy), 168
Flatley, J., 49, 66, 94
FLIP (strategy), 180–181, 182
Flood, J., 50
Floriani, B., 39
Fluent reading
 coral reading and, 82, 84
 paired reading and, 17, 19
Fowler, G., 124
France, I.M., 24
Function words, 9

Galda, L., 105
Gambrell, L., 79
Gammage, S., 144
Gee, T., 124, 149
Gersten, R., 194
Gipe, J., 91, 121
Glover, M., 91
Goldman, M., 79
Goldman, S., 79
Goodman, Y., 114

Goswami, U., 34
Graphemes, 13, 14, 24–25
Graphic
 organizer (strategy), 147–148
 similarity, 5, 52, 82, 147, 173, 180, 181, 189, 200
Graphophonic
 cues, 39
Graves, D., 187
Greenwood, S., 31
GRIP (strategy), 58–59
Group summarizing (strategy), 149–150
Grouping, 45, 60, 61, 114
 cooperative, 23, 149
 partner, 8, 19, 29, 141–142, 153, 164, 169
 small, 21, 41, 113, 175
 teams, 29, 153
Guerra, T., 191
Guided reading procedure (strategy), 93–94, 95
Guide-o-rama (strategy), 94, 96
Gunning, T., 34

Haggard, M., 29
Haidemos, J., 107
Hansen, J., 44
Harrington, S., 161
Heller, M., 98
Herrman, B., 134
Heymsfeld, C., 189
Higdon, P., 23
Higginson, B., 35
Hilbert, S., 120
Hoffbenkoske, K., 31
Hollingsworth, P., 58
Hubler, M., 78, 196

Inductive
 instruction, 13
 phonics (strategy), 13–15
Informal books (strategy), 96–97
Information charts (strategy), 181, 183, 184
Initial sounds, 8, 25
InQuest (strategy), 97–98
Intuitive reading (strategy), 183

Jigsaw method (strategy), 98–99
Johnson, B., 39
Jolly, H., 9
Jones, L., 134
Jongsma, K., 173
Juel, C., 17

Kapinus, B., 64
Keywords (strategy), 59–60
Kinderjournals (strategy), 151–152
King, J., 194
Klemp, R.M., 40
Konopak, B., 59
Koskinen, P., 17, 79
Kreeft, J., 141
KWLA (strategy), 99–100, 101
KWL-Plus (strategy), 100, 103

Lange, J., 195
Langer, J., 188
Lapp, D., 50
Lehnert, L., 39
Lehr, F., 177
Levenson, S., 66
Levesque, J., 57
Lewowicz, N., 8
Linek, W., 169
Linguistic roulette (strategy), 104
List-group-label (strategy), 60–61, 62
Literature circles (strategy), 61, 63
Lombard, M., 113

Making words (strategy), 15–17, 18
Mandeville, T., 99
Mangrum, C., 168, 180, 194
Manning, G., 140
Manning, M., 140
Manzo, A.V., 93, 113
Marginal glosses (strategy), 63
Mateja, J., 60, 94
Matter, E., 135
Matthew, P., 155
Maze, 11
McCauley, G., 82
McCauley, J., 82
McCutchen, D., 24
McKenzie, J., 78
McKenzie, J.V., 196
McLaughlin, E.M., 155
McPherson, M.D., 88
McTague, B., 142
Mead, F., 34
Meaning vocabulary, 8
Mermelstein, B., 175
Middle school picture books (strategy), 153
Morris, D., 23
Moskow, S., 155
Motor imaging (strategy), 64
Mulhall, M., 151

Necaise, M., 91
Nelson, L., 23
Norton, D., 121

Ogle, D., 99, 100
OH RATS (strategy), 185, 187
Olsen, M., 124, 149
Oral language, 27

Padak, N., 17
Paired repeated reading (strategy), 17, 19
Pantomimes, 64. *See also* Motor imaging
Patberg, J., 50
Patterns
    letter, 10, 16, 26, 27
Pearson, P., 44, 97
Perfetti, M.C.A., 24
Perrone, V., 116
Phelan, P., 35
Phoneme, 13, 14, 24–25
Phonemic
    awareness, 8, 10, 13, 15, 21, 26, 34, 39
    elements, 13–15
    patterns, 14
Phonics
    consonant sounds, 14, 15
    decoding, 24
    inductive instruction, 13
    spelling patterns, 16, 17
Phonogram, 19
Playing about a story (strategy), 105
Pointdexter, C., 98
Portfolios (strategy), 105–106
Possible sentences (strategy), 64–65
Predicting, 10, 24, 27, 65, 86, 88, 106, 107, 111, 120, 154, 161, 169, 178, 189, 194, 199
Prediction book report (strategy), 106–107
Predict-o-gram (strategy), 65–66, 67
Prenn, M., 187
Prereading, 31, 35, 37, 40, 52, 61, 65, 113, 116, 134, 149, 154, 170, 175, 178, 179, 196
Preschoolers, 21
Previewing books (strategy), 187–188
Prior knowledge, 37, 49, 61, 65, 99, 116, 122, 135, 172, 180, 193
Probable passages (strategy), 154–155, 156
Progressive cloze (strategy), 19–21
PSRT (strategy), 188–189

Pulliam, C., 108
Purposes for reading, 113, 122
Pyramid (strategy), 66, 68, 69–70
Pyramiding (strategy), 107–108, 109

QAR (strategy), 108, 110
QUIP (strategy), 155, 157, 158

Randall, S., 181
Raphael, T., 44, 108
Read aloud (strategy), 111
Reading
    fluency, 17, 19, 23, 24, 35, 50, 82, 84, 183
    intuitive, 183 (*see also* Intuitive reading (strategy))
    place (strategy), 111–112
    selective (strategy), 193–194
    shared, 45, 120 (*see also* Big books)
Reciprocal teaching (strategy), 189–190
Recoding, 59
Reed, D., 153
Repeated reading (strategy), 112
ReQuest (strategy), 113–114
Reutzel, D., 58, 170
Reviewing a film (strategy), 157, 159, 160
Richards, J., 91, 121
Richards, K., 116
Richek, M., 142
Riley, J., 19
RMA (strategy), 114–115
Robb, L., 26, 96, 106, 144
Robbins, C., 34
Roberts, L., 124
Robinson, B., 132
Robinson, N., 27
Roderick, J., 141
Rodriguez, M., 71
Rutland, A., 49, 66, 94

Sampson, M.B., 169
Sampson, M.R., 169
Sandberg, K., 108
SCAIT (strategy), 190–191, 192
Schlimmer, K., 136
Schneider, M., 132
Schumm, J., 180
Schwartz, R., 44
Scientific method (strategy), 191, 193
Scott, J., 194
Seifert-Kessel, N., 134
Selective reading guide-o-rama (strategy), 193, 194

Semantic
    feature analysis (strategy), 68, 71, 72–74
    mapping, 116–119 (*see also* Conceptual mapping (strategy))
Sentence collecting (strategy), 159
Service, 9. *See also* Connecting words and Function words
Shablak, S., 94, 193
Shanahan, T., 132
Shared book experience (strategy), 120
Sharp, D., 136
Shoop, M., 97
Simons, S., 188
Siu-Runyan, Y., 105
Smith, C., 78
Smith, C.C., 196
Smith, H.M., 153
Smith, S., 97
Smyers, T., 178
Sorrell, A., 131
Sounding out, 25
Sound isolation (strategy), 21–22
Speaker, R., 159
Spiegel, D., 93
SQ3R (strategy), 194–195
SSR (strategy), 120–121
S2RAT (strategy), 195–196
Stahl, N., 194
Stahl, S., 64, 194
Stanovich, K., 142
Stark, C., 130
Stauffer, R.G., 86
Stewart, R., 63
Sticker books (strategy), 23
Story (strategies)
    board, 161, 162
    character map, 121–122, 123
    frames, 124, 126–127, 128–129
    impressions, 122, 124, 125
    retelling, 127
    writing map, 130–131
Story structure
    character elements and, 14, 57, 96, 121, 122, 197
    concept of story and, 66, 68, 189
    plot element in, 57, 88, 122, 142, 197
    point of view element and, 96, 126, 136
    teaching strategies and, 96–97
Strichart, S., 168, 194
Structural analysis, 39
    generalizations, 27
    prefix, 39
    suffix, 39

Summarization (strategy), 131
Support-reading (strategy), 23–24
Surbeck, E., 91
Swan, A., 161
Synthetic phonics (strategy), 24–25

Talking books (strategy), 25–26
Taylor, B., 50, 168
TELLS fact or fiction (strategy), 131–132, 133
Text
    expository, 31, 49, 52, 65, 111, 114, 126, 127, 130, 134, 155, 169, 172, 177, 181, 188, 191, 195, 196, 197, 199
    inferential, 58, 59, 191
    narrative, 31, 49, 52, 104, 111, 114, 126, 130, 134, 136, 170, 172, 177, 191, 195, 199
    preview (strategy), 196–197, 198
    structure (strategy), 197, 199
Thematic
    experience (strategy), 132, 134
    word wall (strategy), 26–27, 28
Think-aloud (strategy), 134–135
Thomas, K., 177
3W2H (strategy), 140–141
Tipton, J., 52
Toast (strategy), 71, 75

Underlining (strategy), 199–200

Vacca, J., 197
Vacca, R., 17, 197
Van Der Voort, T., 79
Visual comprehension (strategy), 135–136
Visual guessing game (strategy), 75–76
VLP (strategy), 27, 29, 30
Vocabulary, 27, 35, 37, 116, 154
    analogies and, 31, 34
    categorization activities, 60, 68, 71
    concept maps, 44, 52
    list group label and, 60, 61
    possible sentences and, 64–65
    self-collection (strategy), 29, 31, 32, 33
    sight, 23, 25, 39, 40, 120
Vowel
    digraphs, 15
    long, 15, 26, 27
    short, 15, 26

Wagon wheels (strategy), 200–201
Walker, B., 122
Webbing (strategy), 136–137
Weissman, K., 100
Wiesendanger, K., 190
Williams, N., 59
Winters, D., 136

Wolf, K., 105
Wood, K., 27, 60, 94, 154
Word
    analogies (strategy), 31, 34
    analysis, 10, 24, 27, 31, 40, 131, 195
    attack, 39
    building, 27, 34–35, 36
    classification, 34
    cluster (strategy), 35, 37, 38
    expansions (strategy), 39
    family, 25
    identification, 10, 17, 27, 40, 82, 114, 142, 195
    meaning, 44, 50, 52, 56, 82, 84
    patterns, 15, 35
    recognition, 24, 142
    sort (strategy), 39–40
    storm (strategy), 40–42
Wordless picture books (strategy), 161, 163
Worthy, M.J., 127
Writing process, 164

Yopp, H., 21

Zig Zag (strategy), 163–165
Zutell, J., 10